TRANSCENDENT
WISDOM OF THE
MAYA

"*Transcendent Wisdom of the Maya* bridges the Western scientific worldview and the spiritual world of the Maya brilliantly. Its wonderful photographs and detailed storytelling are very compelling. I have enjoyed time with the Maya in the Yucatan, and Gabriela's wonderful stories of weaving, dancing, healing, and divining brought it all back to me as if I'd never left. Her description of her welcoming ceremony by the Quiché Maya is a significant contribution to anthropological literature, and the New Era celebration in 2012 offers hope for our future. This is a heartfelt and genuine story of Maya life, a must-read for understanding their time cycles and culture."

BARBARA HAND CLOW, AUTHOR OF *THE MAYAN CODE*
AND *AWAKENING THE PLANETARY MIND*

"Gabriela Jurosz-Landa's rich and enlightening book is a surprising spiritual journey to mysterious cultures, an inner-self journey, and possibly a road map for our culture's future survival. Her destined journey from her native Czechoslovakia to Germany to the United States and Guatemala, where she was initiated as a daykeeper (shaman-priestess), is fascinating. Gabriela generously shares deep knowledge and wisdom of the ancient Maya heritage as she takes us through the process of her initiation. I highly recommend this superb book."

ITZHAK BEERY, AUTHOR OF *THE GIFT OF SHAMANISM* AND
SHAMANIC HEALING AND EDITOR OF *SHAMANIC TRANSFORMATIONS*

"This book brings to life glimpses of the ancient Maya sacred texts and artwork. It is a gift to see their ancient underlying beliefs live on through the Quiché Maya of Chichicastenango."

ERIKA BUENAFLOR, M.A., J.D., AUTHOR OF *CLEANSING RITES*
OF CURANDERISMO AND *CURANDERISMO SOUL RETRIEVAL*

"Ancient Maya culture comes alive in Gabriela Jurosz-Landa's *Transcendent Wisdom of the Maya*. The book offers many insights into centuries-old rituals and spirituality which are still lived today by contemporary Maya. Filled with personal observations from fieldwork, the author presents studious thoughts and goes deep into Maya mythology to contrast the Western worldview."

STUART A. GOLDMAN, EXECUTIVE PRODUCER
OF THE PBS SERIES *JOSEPH CAMPBELL: MYTHOS*

"If you suspect that our technologically proficient culture is losing its soul, then dive into *Transcendent Wisdom of the Maya* where you will find an entrancing alternative to the relentless sense of urgency that dominates our times."

RAND FLEM-ATH, LIBRARIAN AND
COAUTHOR OF *ATLANTIS BENEATH THE ICE*

TRANSCENDENT
WISDOM OF THE
MAYA

The Ceremonies and Symbolism
of a Living Tradition

GABRIELA JUROSZ-LANDA

Bear & Company
Rochester, Vermont

Bear & Company
One Park Street
Rochester, Vermont 05767
www.BearandCompanyBooks.com

Bear & Company is a division of Inner Traditions International

Cataloging-in-Publication Data for this title is available from the Library of Congress

ISBN 978-1-59143-334-7 (print)
ISBN 978-1-59143-335-4 (ebook)

Printed and bound in the United States by McNaughton & Gunn

10 9 8 7 6 5 4 3 2 1

Text design and layout by Priscilla Baker
This book was typeset in Garamond Premier Pro, with Avant Garde and American Brewery used as display typefaces

To send correspondence to the author of this book, mail a first-class letter to the author c/o Inner Traditions • Bear & Company, One Park Street, Rochester, VT 05767, and we will forward the communication, or contact the author directly at **www.gabriela-jurosz-landa.jimdo.com.**

In honor and gratitude to Ahau
And in friendship and gratitude to the
Maya People of Chuwilá

᭬

Hombro a hombro, pies a pies,
descalzos y con cara al sol.
(Shoulder to shoulder, foot to foot,
barefoot and [always] facing the Sun.)

MAYA SAYING

CONTENTS

PART 1

2012—THE END AND THE BEGINNING OF AN ERA

PART 2

DIARY OF LIFE WITH THE MAYA

PART 3

THE SPIRITUAL JOURNEY

FOREWORD

THE FOUNDATIONS OF THE MAYA WORLDVIEW

José Luis Tigüilá NABÉ kaxbaltzij
(Spokesperson of the Maya municipality)

At the closing of the Oxlajuj Baktun on 12/21/12, one era ended, and a new one—the Jun Akabal or Jun Baktun—began. The greatness of the Maya world is based on the wisdom of our ancestors; grandfathers and grandmothers, who left the history embodied in the writings and through the continuity of our spiritual guides, THE AJKIJ,* who give life to it today, those who, with the gift (talent) of the word as a pillar of strength to achieve the defense of the Maya peoples, have begun the copious work of expanding Maya knowledge to offer to the world its first opportunity to get to know a world unknown within the history of the creation of man. [The ancient Maya put their inspiration from the spiritual world into the texts, and today's ajq'ijab—through the same method of receiving messages from the spiritual world—can read what was put into the words back then.]†

---

*José Luis Tigüilá's foreword has been translated from Spanish by the book's author. Maya spellings are based on an interpretation of sounds. For this reason, we have chosen to keep the spellings Mr. Tigüilá has provided. In this foreword, you will also see the use of capitalization preserved as it was submitted for publication.

†Brackets have been used to give further explanation of the text.

The ethical, philosophical, and mystical arguments of the Maya vision of the world and of life in the Maya culture are contained in many sacred books, including the Chilam Balam; the Rabinal Achi; the Codices of Dresden, Madrid, Paris, and Grolier; and especially the Pop Wuj. Strengthening the knowledge of the young indigenous authorities [by passing the ancestral knowledge on to them because the young indigenous authorities are educated mostly in the Western way and the elders are soon to be gone] is the means to knowledge for the world and future generations. The interlocution [exchange of knowledge from the elder generation to the younger] validates the full effort of the practiced traditions [those of the spoken word, action, traditions, and usage] as they were followed through millennia by the Maya people. There is evidence that to the Maya people the universe is a system of systems—systems in which diverse and autonomous units are articulated.

The grandfathers and grandmothers gathered under the shadow of AJAW (God) initiated the PIXAP* to decide whether the knowledge of the Maya people should remain immersed in anonymity and be called all kinds of adjectives, such as INDOLENT, ILLITERATE, IGNORANT [as has been the case], or whether it was time to present the ancestral knowledge embedded in each of the sons of the Maya people, who have received the strength of the knowledge orally and through experiential living. The result of the great PIXAP was to start the process of extracting knowledge from the elders and present it to all people who want to learn about the Maya world, and especially to those who want to understand the Maya philosophy—to understand the Maya world, you must think like a Maya.

---

*The Pixap is the Maya council that meets to discuss matters of the various Maya communities. December 21, 2012, was a renewal of the tradition, and elders from different Maya communities gathered in Chichicastenango. The ancient sources of the ancestors indicated that after future centuries of darkness [that have now passed], their descendants should open the ancestral knowledge to people besides/outside of the Maya ajq'ijab.

WE DO NOT STUDY THE POP VUH,
WE WRITE AND LIVE THE POP VUH.
WE DO NOT STUDY THE MAYA CODICES,
WE WRITE AND LIVE THE MAYA CODICES.
WE NEED TO STRIVE TO THE FUTURE,
    FOOT BY FOOT, SHOULDER BY
    SHOULDER, FACING THE SUN AND
    WIND, BAREFOOTED, BUT WITH
    SECURE STEP.

JOSÉ LUIS TIGÜILÁ, 2018

ACKNOWLEDGMENTS

First and foremost, my gratitude goes to my Creator and the protectors of my life (some of whom are Maya).

During my many years of involvement with the people in Guatemala, I met at least two people each day to be grateful to for allowing me to share a piece of their lives. That is a lot of people to consider, and in my heart I do so.

Explicitly, my heart and gratitude will always go to Don Tomás Calvo Mateo, the Quichéan leader who invited me to the 2012 celebrations and many others thereafter, took me on official encounters with the Guatemalan government and Maya regional leaders, granted me physical and spiritual protection, and, though we could only talk through our hearts or interpreters, taught me how to be grateful in the first place. Don Tomás passed on in October 2017. May he rest in peace.

I am also indebted to my wonderful Nana Tomasa Pol Suy and her daughter Nana Sebastiana, who urged me to take the spiritual path of the Maya and led me through the process with love and feminine sensitivity.

I am grateful to Manuel Xiloj, the leader's right hand, for taking me under his wing. His sudden passing at a young age—one month after the chief's death—remains a mystery. My friend, you are greatly missed. I thank his sister Josefa Xiloj for her friendship and support; José Luis Tigüilá for his eloquent teachings and friendship;

the Maya administration's lawyer, Julio David Diaz Chay, for the intellectual-cultural insights he shared with me; and all the people of Chichicastenango for one way or another letting me participate in the life of their town.

I thank my supportive partners during the years of this journey, which is far from over.

I thank Professor Ferdinand Anders at the University of Vienna for portraying the Maya culture in a vivid way. I also thank my editors, Antoinette LeRoux, Jill Rogers, and Kayla Toher.

I thank my mother for being a liberal though strict educator and philosopher who, by example and in nightly conversations, opened a mental world to me that few are granted. I thank my father, who introduced me to the world of adventure and fostered courage above all.

In an abstract way, I thank Comenius, the grand Czech philosopher whose naturalistic conception of education has given me the means of explaining events and situations so that readers can experience them as if they were their own.

PREFACE

WIDENING THE
SCOPE OF SCIENCE

In the field of anthropology today, we encounter a multitude of theories that lack the ability to translate the findings of academia to application in actual reality, an objective in any human activity. Deeply revering the educative principles of the social reformer Comenius,* who was a proponent of practical universal education and delineated a teaching method that proposed the gradual learning of comprehensive, *practicable* concepts, I decided to write this book from a less theoretical and more evocative and personal perspective. Having had the opportunity to actively dive into Maya spiritual practice as a shaman-priestess initiate, my anthropologic contribution is to give insight into contemporary Maya life and its philosophy, customs, and spiritual practices as they are vibrantly lived today within an unchanged cosmology that has been transmitted from ancient Maya times. Along with this lively portrait of real Maya life, it is also my desire to present a viable alternative to the current Western philosophy by offering axioms for intercultural comparison.

Claude Lévi-Strauss, Margaret Mead, Franz Boas, and many older and younger anthropologists experienced uncanny occurrences when

---

*For more about Comenius, visit The State University Education Encyclopedia website page on "Johann Comenius" (1592–1670).

they exposed themselves to foreign societies. Their experiences in the field, however, have been taken to be less important than their rationalized theoretical conclusions. As I see it, in the study of consciousness giving testimony of one's experiencing something or gaining insight into someone else's experience and living it to an extent is valuable and true to reality compared with context-limited theories. Recent anthropological theories and methods have contributed greatly to the advancement of the discipline. The explanation, interpretation, and conceptualization of these theories, however, still leaves open questions: Do the conclusions lead to a deeper understanding of reality, and are they universally applicable to society?

The answer comes down to substance, physical and metaphysical, touchable (material) or possible to experience via other senses than touch (metaphysical "matter"), which results through the mythos of life. Ultimately, most traditional and contemporary theories formed up until now have largely ignored the metaphysical core of anthropology. For fear of colliding with the rational principles of science, recent anthropology is still caving in to seeking no more than partial knowledge and in doing so betrays its raison d'être, which lies in studying people to understand their ways of thinking and living. The task of our discipline should always be to link observed behavior to the inner workings of a culture and compare them to Western thought. Why else study behavior, if not to understand it and relate it to the principles of one's own thought to extend and enrich one's life, and in the process rescue knowledge that once was as common in Europe as it is in traditional societies today? It is here where science and modern spirituality intersect. Physicists admit that they have not so far reached ontological awareness of our time-space existence and operate on only partial knowledge. Science, without metaphysics, cannot come to true results unless it defines these results exclusively as findings of physical reality. To do this, science separates physical reality from nonphysical reality. To enrich the future of science, I consider it essential to widen its scope to include spiritual science and experience so as to create a dialogue. Without openness to accepting spiritual knowledge of native peoples as a core of knowing about man, and without translating this knowledge for the realm of rational science, anthropology will never get out of the corner it has backed itself into, where it is hiding instead of leading. If anthropology cannot hold up its significance as a science because spirituality is not rationally provable, and if the field of science in the twenty-first century, where we talk about the relativity of time and space, more-dimensionality, and even multiverses, cannot be extended to something researching the unprovable even though it is a fundamental part of being human, anthropology might want to consider forming a discipline that permits advancement into a space beyond.

Ideally, Western science will consider two approaches. One is to reclaim pre-Christian philosophical concepts, the other is to broaden its study to include non-Western cosmologies, including their metaphysical dimensions, to advance its understanding of the dynamism of time and space that quantum physics has already begun to discover. To do so, science may want to open itself to a different method, one that phenomenology or metametaphysics, if extended to further disciplines, could possibly provide.

By phenomenological means, which studies "objects" through direct experience, this book will provide a view into Maya consciousness by showing examples of the real and everyday practices of the Maya people, who have managed to preserve much that the Inquisition made extinct in Europe and elsewhere. This work attempts to reconstruct the spiritual parts of life that have been lost in Western culture due to its gradual rationalization.

Many people educated in Westernized societies are currently realizing the limits of Western rationalism. Aiming to reconnect to a holistic life experience, they search for spiritual engagement and its connection to daily life. I was given the opportunity to experience such a connection while living with the Maya spiritual caste and "ordinary" people who vividly and constantly communicated with their higher-ups in heaven, as our ancestors used to be able to do. In a give-and-take relationship, they cherished God, the saints, and the numinous energies that dwell among them. In doing so, they receive support from these entities in return.

Trapped in a world of convenience, many of us today have lost touch with this network of nature and the universe. Whether or not you recognize this lost connection, I hope this book will help you encounter or enhance your own spiritual life.

INTRODUCTION

THE CONTEMPORARY SEARCH FOR MEANING

Christianity triumphed in the world and became a universal religion only because it detached itself from the climate of the Greco-Oriental mysteries and proclaimed itself a religion of salvation accessible to all.

When religious historian Mircea Eliade wrote the above words in 1958 (Eliade 2012, 17), a new, globalized society was already under way. Questioning the status quo, politically as well as spiritually, and in light of a globalized life, many people began to incorporate other religions and spiritual practices into the one with which they grew up. Who would have thought that so many people would abandon the church of their heritage, and who could have envisioned that a practice such as yoga would become mainstream in the West? On the verge of economic and political globalization, Western people today once again request spiritual holism—possibly one that, independent of cultural and geographical separation, would one day unite people around the globe.

Today, people in industrialized societies lack the idea of a unified world. They live in a dual world, at most. While physically occupying the natural world, one also inhabits a world proposed by science and its prolongation—technology. Occupying a position of dominance in Western daily life, the concept of the machine tends to overrun

1

humanity. A redefinition of humanity as a hybrid of natural being and machine is already in progress. The microchip, the Sofia robot, and the Watson or Tianhe supercomputers are starting to infiltrate the mass media and with it our homes.

With life divided into specialized sectors, the essential sense of life unity once provided by spirituality and/or religion has been lost for many. A new philosophical or spiritual infrastructure, or "Überbau," to hold together the different fabrics and worlds of life today has not yet been created. But a new search for meaning is under way, and people in the modern world are looking to churches and tribal spirituality for answers.

People travel to the Amazon to learn from the shamans or to India to practice yoga to expand their minds' capacities. They delve deeper into the knowledge of the people and nature of the Himalayas, and they replace conventional diet and medicine with their organic and holistic equivalents.

In the meantime, in our universities, young scientists from different fields studying the Self are still learning to oppose the idea of morality (psychology) versus memory (neuroscience). Examining a phenomenon from an extreme perspective consequently leads to extraneous ideas that are equally extreme. Not surprising is the fact that exploring spirituality scientifically may lead to the judgment that everything nonscientific is suspicious, a notion bundled in the terms *mystical* and *occult*. These unsatisfyingly ambiguous terms do not express the natural quality of their content.

To the nonscientist, there is nothing mystical about any form of conversation with God or numinous beings—whether in so-called tribal context or via world religions. Rather than touching the heart, contemporary science often points a finger, and most of the time true mind and common sense fall to scientific rational limitation, which today quite often has a heartless and inhuman demeanor that easily binds with the emotionless machine.

But how should people who are little educated in matters of the heart, and who move ever deeper toward a mechanized reality, even recognize their lack of understanding and awareness? The dividing discourse of contemporary science tends to neglect the question of what unites humans with each other and with their surroundings, because the answer to such a question is not measurable.

That which is sacred tends to unite. So how does the definition of *human being*, as a unifying entity, fit into today's scientist's perception? "Self" and "thought," two of the foremost ideas explored by psychology, have been defined distinctly by many throughout history. By studying the Greek author Homer, we notice that he did not define a gap between thinking and feeling (Rappe 1995, 75). This opposition to the Western post-Greek worldview (more specifically post-Descartes) needs adjusting. One cannot find a true orientation in the world when looking at thinking and feeling as two separate concepts disconnected from each other. For when these entities are separated, one becomes easy prey for manipulation. Unfortunately, those who are able to unify the spirituality of thinking and feeling are sometimes seen as a threat and can become the subjects of persecution.*

Universally, people's reactions and decisions primarily originate from what Czech phenomenologist Jan Patočka called the "natural world," which is originally and intrinsically a part of reality that is tied to human nature. Not able to withstand the pressure of critical thinking, we stopped trusting our basic instinct. John Amos Comenius, and here is our connection to the Maya, showed the importance of returning to understanding the essences of phenomena—simply their original and true meaning, which in Western society today often gets lost or diluted. We can easily do so through thinking, and we reach satisfactory results when thinking and feeling are unified and make a trine with the spiritual realm. Comenius's method is to start out simple and gradually tie in more complex learning without losing the connection to the essential

---

*For instance, the Chinese government incarcerates practitioners of Falun Gong, a practice that combines qigong with Taoist moral teachings.

meaning or, as Patočka would call it, the natural world. This process is not a one-way street. It requires stretching the muscle of reflexivity, as thinking and living are reflexive processes. But many Westerners today do not actively stop to consider the world around them or experience it fully. Having lost control of spirituality over time, Westerners today inhabit a matrix in which they are subject and victim to scientific and marketing paradigms. Gradually, more and more power is taken from them by a power-holding minority.

The value of spiritual unity between humans and nature, the trophy of creation, has splintered, and many Westerners now rank at the level of mere goods. In a fragmented world, people may have impressions, observations, thoughts, and memories, but these singular pieces do not form a unified reality, a dynamic world that is alive and subjective (Patočka 1992, 98). Instead of creating their own spirituality, the masses nowadays choose advertised ideas and follow the teachings and movements of an instructor, such as a celebrity preacher or yoga teacher.

According to phenomenologists, understanding things out of our personal perception is an ability based in the natural world. Science, on the contrary, aims to objectivize the world. The natural world, however, cannot contain what is not objectively explainable. Therefore, it cannot function as a counterargument for objectivism.

Rationality removes humans from their original, natural Self so that a large part of their actions and thoughts are alienated from their nature. Since Descartes, we have been told that rationality is the path to the Self, whereas in reality it is only when the Self is rooted in nature that it can make sense of the world. That process of "sense-making" involves all the senses, including those not of the mind and its tools of rationality. The scientific process that crept into the general understanding of the world, inundated by the pretentious world of advertising and the inescapable role models of the film and TV industry, slices up the unity of the world without creating what Jan Patočka (1992, 98) would call a "net of interactions" that causes a discrepancy that Patočka sees as a crisis of the soul in humans. A world filled with objectivity does not allow people to feel free to make spontaneous decisions or to choose based on interest, away from outside pressure. People living in such a system often perceive freedom, but because their Self is often not rooted in its natural foundation, it has been subjected to outside forces. People start seeing themselves as objects rather than human beings (Patočka 1992, 5). This perception alienates people from their natural Self even further, causing them to finally give up on themselves and start adhering to and relying on the guidance of outer forces—such as the gym instructor, a TV persona, the chef in a cooking show, or a political leader—and unconsciously disintegrating their natural identity and forming one that is alien to their natural being. This sounds like a dark picture, but to many it is real.

The Maya, too, live in a dual, if not a quadruple, world.* Theirs, however, is bound together by mythical substance. Based on—and accepting—their common primary events and their resulting history (which in many ways is the repetition of the primary events), as well as spirituality and a daily life bound to nature, the traditional Maya strive for unity rather than divergence. Their objective is not to abandon or change what their forefathers planted but to be as true to it as possible and to respect the judgment of their forefathers. Because they believe that those ancestors received direct instructions from the Creator(s), they consider that knowledge to be pure (or close to pure). Maya "repetition of the primary events" is essential for ensuring that their origin will not be lost, and it serves as the basis for complex thought. This concept correlates with Comenius's "tying together basic thought and complex multitude." Complexity results from simplicity.

As to unity cracked open into multiple forms, the Maya recognize both as existing in one and the same realm of existence. That means that every complex thought can be related to its origin. The traditional Maya recognize the need for change to keep things moving, and historic

---

*Recall how Mr. Tigüilá stated in the foreword of this book that there is evidence that the universe is a system of systems to the Maya people—systems in which diverse and autonomous units are articulated.

events such as the European Conquest shook up and changed their lives profoundly. Nevertheless, they relate and weigh every change against the primordial event, holding the consciousness alive. In this way, their rituals and customs ultimately serve to keep the world together. Without a balance between fragmentation and unity and without a unifying philosophy, the world could disintegrate in a way that humans could not handle.

Meanwhile, many Westerners have mocked and discarded this sacred connection. Some even demean altogether the idea of a personal or impersonal Creator or energy who gave humans a blueprint.

Since communication between the Creator's forces and human beings is mostly nonverbal, humans need to be in tune with a variety of forms of communication to understand this blueprint. They must also level their energy and its frequency with that of the numinous being(s) in order to make contact possible. Traditional societies, such as the Maya, have specialists who cultivate this knowledge of communication. They live and heal by listening to the input of higher forces through the method we call "shamanism." In a lecture titled "Why Shamanism Works," given at Yale University in April 2017, Jan van Alphen summarized how the art of convincing influences the brain.

> Most illnesses are mental. This fact has been repeated, the reason however has not. Among the various dimensions of the human body, the head is the seat of the brain. The brain is central to the human body, because it manages all other body parts. The organs function due to decisions in the brain. Their vital energy is determined there. The brain holds the major power over all human endeavors, well-being, and his overall existence. So how is it that we doctor the different parts of the body instead of impinging on the brain? It is that simple.
>
> To influence the brain, frequencies work. Sound, color, light, fragrances, and ultimately love. A voice can speak affirmative prayers, a drum produces full and round sounds, a bag of seeds creates a sound

like ants leaving the body. Pleasant colors and fragrances over time affect the brain and can transform its stuck beliefs. If someone else can convince you of something, your brain is convinced. The art of the shaman is ultimately the art of convincing. Otherwise, one is stuck believing that the physician can do better.

Shamanism is known to be well advanced in the nonphysical realm of brain function, something Western medicine tends to ignore. As anthropologists, we explore foreign cultures for comparison with our own. A major part of our discipline involves the study of medicinal plants, and shamanism can help to bridge the gap between native shamanic practice and Western medicine.

My Maya journey started with visions in childhood that led me to study anthropology and to live in Guatemala, meet the leader of the Maya Quiché, and dive into the practice of cultural-spiritual traditions by observation, participation, and initiation. Part 1 of this book describes my encounter with the Maya Highest Authority and the 2012 turning of time. The spiritual-cultural expression in that weeklong event demonstrated Maya cosmology and how Maya life is based on calendars. The first part of the book also introduces my concept of time, backed by the Maya perception. Part 2 focuses on daily life, which is based on calendrical spiritual principles, as well as other ritual events I was invited to attend. Part 3 recounts the day-to-day process of my initiation in 2015 as a Maya shaman-priestess according to the Maya Cholq'ij calendar.

Throughout my university studies, I realized that the goal of anthropological work should be to combine the originally common fundamental principles and their expressions in other cultures with the Western way of life in order to reconstruct some of what was lost by historic developments—such as the Inquisition and Enlightenment—when rationality raged through Europe and the world. The compared cultures can learn from, enrich, and perhaps even heal each other. I would argue that if Western culture would put more effort into sowing science into society spiritually instead of speeding off in the name of progress and only making sense of the world on a limited rational basis, humanity would be more whole and live its existence the way it was designed to be lived. Though Spirit often needs time, which does not fit into the contemporary idea of effectiveness, hopefully modern humanity will take this direction.

Map of Guatemala showing Chichicastenango, where I lived while completing my research. Used with permission from worldatlas.com.

PART 1

2012—THE END AND THE BEGINNING OF AN ERA

1

A JOURNEY INTO MAYA HISTORY AND TRADITION

When Don Tomás Calvo Mateo gave me a big smile and invited me to attend the celebrations of the New Era in Guatemala, I knew that I would embark on a journey that would lead me into the past and future—mine and that of an eternal, even mythical, people.

I met Don Tomás in New York City. At that time he was accepted by many Maya groups as the highest authority of the Maya people in Guatemala. It was in October 2012 when he, accompanied by his administrative team, came to visit New York for the first time, having been invited by an organization called Maya Now. They had planned various appearances at the UN, New York University, and Central Park, some of which had to be canceled because of Hurricane Sandy.

My meeting them happened by chance—or by prediction. In 2001, still living in Guatemala, I dreamed that I would frequent many airports for twelve "levels of a hotel," which I interpreted as twelve years. After that, I would return to the Maya pyramids. It happened exactly like that.

Living in New York, it took me three years to stop being homesick for Guatemala, where I had spent a good part of six years between 1995 and 2001. After that the idea of exploring the spiritual traditions in an anthropological and personal manner slowly subsided and didn't cross my mind for many years, until one specific day . . .

I was in a neighborhood café getting some sun, which was rare among the skyscrapers in NoHo, New York. Sipping my morning coffee, I noticed a man at the table next to me, reading a book on the Maya. It then struck me that too many years had passed since I had thought of Maya life, and that I should look into the matter again. Having been a "typical New Yorker" for some time, I had embraced my scholarly existence as an art critic more than my existence as an anthropologist trained in Maya culture and had been covering art for European magazines for several years.

I went home that day thinking that I should contact the Maya Elders. I had never had any particular personal contact with the leaders of the Maya or with any of the shamans in Guatemala. I did have an Austrian friend who had lived in Guatemala for eighteen years and had been initiated into Maya shamanism. Back in 1999, I ran a gallery in her building complex in Antigua, Guatemala. We had seen each other on and off in Vienna, where she lived now, and now the thought crossed my mind to get in touch with her. Antigua is a colonial mestizo town surrounded by Maya villages and filled with the presence of Maya people who come to sell their goods and buy other, needed ones. Today it is frequented by many tourists and is home to many expats.

My friend had left Guatemala when her daughter was kidnapped in 2001, and so had I. In spite of the peace treaty that was signed between the government and the guerrilla groups in 1996, danger still lurked in the streets. Strolling passersby often entered my gallery, and sometimes they were unnerving; a stranger followed me home one night, because he knew where I lived. A sculpture got stolen, and my friend's daughter was kidnapped. The sixteen-year-old girl was released in a public Dumpster, and she made her way back home. But her kidnapping was the last straw for this friend and for me. Having had enough of being afraid all the time, I left Guatemala and began a new life in New York City.

I ended up not asking my friend as I was not comfortable asking friends for favors. As it turned out, reaching out to her was not necessary. From the New York café, I went upstairs into the loft on Great Jones Street, where I lived at the time. At my computer, I opened my emails and saw an invitation from New York University, featuring the visit of Don Tomás Calvo Mateo, the Maya leader, on his first-time visit to New York. Even today I am still in the dark as to how they got my email address and why they sent me notices. Don Tomás's whole schedule was listed, from the UN visit that afternoon to a ceremonial appearance on an open field at Central Park the next Saturday. I was stunned. I could only think, "God responded fast, even without having asked him for anything." I spent the day in a haze, organizing while trying to make sense of the email.

I was due to leave the house in the early evening to meet a photographer friend who had come from Prague to photograph New York bridges for a photo book. Descending the stairs, I met my upstairs neighbor Itzhak Beery by chance. Although Itzhak is now a respected healer, the founder of the New York Shamanic Circle, and the author of three books, he was not yet famous at that time. I only knew that he was some sort of a shaman, educated in the jungles of Ecuador. Until that day, in the fifteen years we lived in the same building, we had never talked much, and the stairs are just too narrow and strenuous to allow for meaningful encounters.

In this chance meeting on the stairs of one building in a city of eight million people, I said to him, "I suppose you know that the Maya leader is in town?" He looked at me and, showing me the bundle on his shoulder hiding a drum in a bag, said, "Yes, that is where I am going right now, to the UN" The UN meeting, as I found out later, included only a handful of people, and I had actually met one of them during that split-second meeting on the stairs to my apartment.

What Itzhak and I didn't know was in what bizarre circumstances we were soon to become friends. I didn't go that day, or the next, but

I did go to the gathering in Central Park. I expected that many people would show up for the appearance of the Maya leader. After all, Don Tomás was to the Maya what the Dalai Lama is to Buddhists.

However, as it turned out, there hadn't been a lot of PR for Don Tomás. When I got to the park, a small group of people were preparing for him by setting up a circle on a hilltop. I tried to introduce myself but quickly realized that these organizers were a tight group of people, not very open to outsiders. I stayed to the side and didn't even speak much to Itzhak, who was with the organizers.

At some point, Don Tomás appeared with three men dressed in traditional clothes and one in a suit from the 1970s. The one in the suit stayed to the side, two of the others took a position outside the circle, observing the group from the back, and the third translated into Spanish what Don Tomás was saying in Quiché, which included a greeting, a thanking, and a message for the future. Then Don Tomás swung a jar with incense back and forth and walked to each of the participants and sanctified us individually with prayers.

As the leader performed his prayers, the man in the suit, Julio David Diaz Chay, addressed me, pulling me out of the group. We spoke in Spanish. He didn't seem surprised when I told him that I had lived in Guatemala and had been to Chichicastenango. I didn't tell him how scared I was there, some fifteen years before, one night when I observed the strange processions of feathered icons among a crowd of Maya people in the scarcely lit narrow streets. Julio David introduced me to Don Tomás and the other Maya men, and Don Tomás invited me to the nightly ceremony at the photographer's house where they were staying for the ten days of their visit. And so I went.

I arrived on time. The little yard behind the town house was filled with chairs and people, but one seat in the first row was vacant. So I sat in it as if it had been reserved for me. The translator from the Central Park gathering turned out to be not only the scribe but also Don Tomás's right hand. He had been educated at a Belgian university as an engineer and was fluent in three languages and some English. He came up to me while assisting Don Tomás with the initiation of the ceremony. As is the Maya tradition, he thanked me for coming.

The leader started talking into the fire while swinging a jar with incense over the flames, which lit up the dark Manhattan night. Later he invited a young Guatemalan mestizo couple over and honored them before the fire. I did not know what was going on, but somehow he was binding them to do or be something throughout the rest of their lives—a very Maya thing to do.

I found out later that the young woman worked at the UN, and Don Tomás and his team thought that she could be of some assistance to further the Maya cause at the UN. What they didn't know was that she actually worked in the African division and had nothing to do with Guatemala besides being Guatemalan herself. After the ceremony there was a reception in the house. We took photos with each other and were happy in each other's company—the Maya and the Westerners and me, who felt like something in between.

After most of the people had left, I offered to show Don Tomás and his group around town. He and the two older men were tired and stayed at the town house, but the two younger people and some of the organizing Maya Now group came along in their minibus. Naturally, I took them to Times Square. Julio David and I walked while conversing and lost contact with the group. As we walked the streets of Manhattan, oblivious to the fluorescent lights and street noise and in a world in between time and space, he told me a lot about Maya life and traditions, and I wondered what anyone could possibly learn about that culture at a university alone or even by living in a town of mixed cultures, as I had.

Around 1:00 a.m., at Bryant Park, I put him into a taxi and sent him back to the photographer's house to get some sleep. The next day, Hurricane Sandy struck. Downtown, we had no electricity, and there was no way to get uptown. The subway was inundated, and the few buses that ran were overcrowded. The rain stopped two days later, and I had had enough of being stuck downtown.

I had no money for the long—and in those days of emergency, ridiculously overpriced—cab ride uptown, so I took the bus. The ride, normally twenty minutes, took two hours. When I got to the photographer's house, the Maya were overjoyed to see me. Don Tomás was attending to "patients" in a room downstairs, and I offered to translate his words into English. People had come from all over to be healed by Don Tomás. So it was the three of us—Don Tomás, Manuel Xiloj (the general manager, as his Quiché title translates into English), and me.

One patient was a young gay man. Don Tomás knew just by looking at him and the candle before him that he had lost his mother at a young age. Another one was a father, who Don Tomas advised to spend more time with his children. He advised most of his patients to light a candle at home, sit before it, ask a question, and wait for the answer to emerge. All of them left very content and calm.

After the meeting we talked late into the night and went out to a nearby bar where their traditional attire drew a lot of attention. By then, I had accepted my best friend's invitation to leave the downtown area, where there was still no electricity and we were lighting a fire to heat the place, and stay in her uptown apartment overnight. It was an interesting moment in New York history, because people had no access to their computers and phones. Some people whom I talked to were recalling life as it was before the technological explosion. To them the moment in time felt like déjà-vu. To me, the perception of time was suspended between the city's rat-race pace of life and that of Maya eternity. I didn't know it as I rode out of the downtown area, but before long, I would find myself out of the rat race and back on a bus, only this time, I would be back in Guatemala and fully immersed in the Maya eternity.

After studying anthropology while attending university in Munich and Vienna, I moved to Guatemala, where I lived for six years in the 1990s. During those years I learned how some people lived integrated with Mother Nature, while others didn't at all. In my daily life in the colonial town of Antigua, I designed jewelry for European designers, painted, and opened a gallery showcasing Western and Guatemalan art.

This daily occupation gave me time to adjust to the culture in a natural way as a resident. My daily life sometimes led me into the mountain region where people lived the Maya way. My life partner, though, was a Guatemalan artist, who lived according to the Maya principles of nature, which he had absorbed as a child from his father. Experiencing the differences between his approach and my Western upbringing filled my days with a profound insight into the Maya worldview. I had several spiritual experiences in those years but didn't meet any of the "pure" Maya, let alone a shaman, for a long time.

I was familiar with the country's beauty and its loving people who were hospitable, friendly, embracing, and above all warmhearted, but sadly I had also experienced various rough encounters involving an underlying current of cruelty—which was to a large degree the result of human nature and several centuries' worth of antagonism, discrimination, and animosity directed by Spanish invaders and local guerrilla warriors—and wars with their diverse pre-Columbian neighbors.

Six hundred years ago the Spanish Conquest eliminated many of the Maya people. Those who were able to escape the cruelty of one of the most rigid and relentless genocides of all time fled into the highlands and still continue to exist as an ethnic community of Maya.

Guatemala was caught up in civil guerrilla warfare from 1960 (the beginning of the Guatemalan Civil War) until approximately 1996, when the peace treaty was signed. The government forces of Guatemala were condemned globally for committing genocide against the Maya population of Guatemala during the civil war and for widespread human rights violations against civilians. Although life started to normalize, the new post-dictator freedom led to a high crime rate within the society.

Thanks to an invitation from Don Tomás after our meeting in New York, the next phase of my life in Guatemala was centered in the town of Chichicastenango (which was called Chuwilá before the Spanish Conquest), up in the Western Highlands in the region of El Quiché. The town is also affectionately known as Santo Tomás, reflecting the name of one of the town's patrons, Saint Thomas. As the spiritual patron of the Maya here, Santo Tomás is embraced by Maya who converted to Christianity, as well as by those who believe in Ahau (God).

Boasting a population of about 150,000 people, Chichicastenango is today's center of the living Maya Quiché, one of the largest ethnic groups in the country. Although the numbers of the Maya community were greatly reduced during the civil war that stretched across more than forty years of the twentieth century, this sad era of their history did not succeed in reducing them to extinction. Quite the contrary. An estimated 65 percent of today's Guatemalan population is still Maya, and despite brutal Christian scrutiny, much of the Maya religion and cosmology has survived and lives on in oral tradition and daily practice.

Chichicastenango lies at an altitude of 6,447 feet in the Guatemalan Highlands and is located about 87 miles northwest of Guatemala City. It is home to the Maya municipality of Quiché, which, until his death in October 2017, was led by Don Tomás Calvo Mateo.

Even beyond the borders of El Quiché, Don Tomás was respected as the highest moral and ancestral authority of the Maya. He was head of the Order of the Maya Lords, who are the Keepers of the Popol Vuh, the Quichéan Maya Book of Council. Don Tomás was predestined by his birth-day energy (I'll explain more about this in later chapters), his family lineage, and his years of dedicated work for the community to be the political leader (highest judge) and spiritual leader.

In conjunction with a highly structured group of Elders, Don Tomás was the Keeper of Maya Knowledge and Tradition. He was also the people's main spiritual guide and the juridical institution in Maya law and administration. Individuals, community leaders, and even the Guatemalan national government looked to him for advice and consulted him accordingly.

The market is the first area that visitors see when they enter the town of Chichicastenango. It embraces the town center and extends into many of the residential side streets. This makes things difficult at times for the residents, but it is condoned by all since business is one of the most vital aspects of Maya existence. Hundreds of items and hard-earned quetzales (the Guatemalan currency) change hands from 6:00 a.m. to about 6:00 p.m. every day in the tightly adjoining shops. (For a photo of the Market Santo Tomás, see plate 1.)

In the market, women interact dressed in their traditional brightly embroidered *huipiles,* or blouses, enshrined by their long, shiny black hair that is braided or held together with glittery pins. Together with men and children they sell a variety of fresh and dried food, candles, flowers, pots, shoes, and all sorts of herbs and spices with which delicious Guatemalan dishes are prepared.

This heart-of-the-town's business district lies in an open space between two churches: Santo Tomás in the east and, directly across from it, in keeping with Christian tradition, the smaller Calvary in the west. The stairs leading up to the churches are the entryways to the sacred ground of the former Maya deity, who was transferred to nearby Pascual Abaj. In many cases, the church steps are the actual steps of the former Maya pyramids, which were replaced by the Christian churches built on top of them. On the steps of the main church, Santo Tomás, a fire is kept burning at all times, prayers are offered, and flowers are sold. Some buy the flowers for home decoration, but most buy them to place on personal or public altars as offerings to the saints.

Though Chichicastenango is not known as a Maya spiritual center, in 2012, Guatemala, and Chichicastenango as the seat of the Quichéan Maya administration, became the center of the world's passage into a new future.

2

2012–"THE END OF THE WORLD"

As a result of the misinterpretation of the Maya prophecies, 2012 was looked upon by scores of people globally as the year in which the world would come to an end. Those very same people can now attest to the fact that they had prepared for something that didn't happen . . . at least not in the way that they had presumed it would.

What clearly influenced so many people into believing that time had run out for humanity was the fact that certain media entities in the Western world misrepresented the true meaning of the Maya end-of-the-world predictions, and sensationalism was probably behind it. A newspaper headline declaring "Tomorrow the World Will End" is bound to sell countless more papers in a day than an ordinary post about day-to-day living could sell in a week.

So what does the "end of the world" really mean in terms of the Maya predictions?

While it is true that the Maya Cholq'ij calendar was not written in stone to extend beyond December 21, 2012, the Maya never cease to calculate time. There is no "end" in a cyclic worldview. Time is central in the consciousness of the Maya, and they begin and end many cycles within their timekeeping system by undertaking rituals rather than fixing things in writing. In the Western world, too, these cycles are known as calendars. From this perspective, it should be clear that the discontinuation of the physical updating of the Cholq'ij calendar did not mean that the Maya did not see any future for themselves (or humanity) after December 21, 2012. As we will see, endings in Maya cosmology are not final, as they are in the Western worldview. December 21, 2012, postulated an "apocatastasis," or the completion of the "Great Year." At once closing and beginning time, the cosmic incident is a renewal.

According to the Popol Vuh (the Maya Book of Creation, or Book of Council), four cycles, or creations, occurred in the past. In each cycle, the Creator and the Framer tried a different approach to create man as a sustainable being. The Maya count, the ajq'ij practice of counting time to show respect for its day energies and to keep the relationship alive with them so as to continue to receive their messages, preserved in this Book of Council as well as in oral memory, looks back thousands of years, stretching the Western concept of human existence way beyond the limits of modern historic education and imagination. Since most people in the industrialized world are not trained to deal with large historic numbers, acknowledging the Maya science often fuels confusion.

The inscription on Stele C at Quiriguá, an archaeological site close to the Guatemalan Atlantic coast, shows a date equivalent to December 21, 2012, in the Western world's Gregorian calendar as the end date of the Maya fourth cycle. This is the only remaining evidence showing the specific time that that cycle would end, a fact that probably caused media uproar in countries far away from Guatemala. The confusion is attributed to the different concepts of time in Western and Maya perception. Within the Maya cyclic concept, there is no ending, no apocalypse. Things always keep going, though within a new cycle. From the Maya perspective, December 21, 2012, ended the Maya fourth cycle and simultaneously began the Maya fifth cycle, also called the Fifth Sun (in Maya Quiché it is called the Job Ahau).

As calculated in the Maya Long Count (Nim Haab) calendar, each of the five cycles, or creations, amounts to 5,125.36 years. Nim means "one" or "the one." In the Gregorian calendar, the date that corresponds to the culmination and end of the fourth of the 5,125.36-year cycles, which began on August 13, 3114 BCE, is December 21, 2012. For the Maya observers of time, that date initiated an even larger cycle of 26,000 years and began a new era.

According to Don Tomás and the Quichéan shaman-priests, the Thirteenth B'aqtun (Oxlajuj B'aqtun) of the Long Count calendar ended at 12:02 on December 21, 2012, Guatemalan time, when, for the first time in 26,000 years, the winter solstice sun passed before the galactic equator, crossing the Center of the galaxy, which the Maya call "Heart of Sky" and which runs north to south. What was significant in 2012 was that also crossing the ecliptic was a series of additional planets, including Earth, running east to west, and when the sun aligned with the Center of the galaxy, the "Cross of the Sky" was created. This cosmic cross is considered to be an embodiment of the Sacred Tree, the Tree of Life—a tree that has significance in many of the spiritual traditions of the world.

Even today, when numerous societies have been violently secularized, many cultures still recognize this event that, according to ancient Maya astronomers, happens only once every 26,000 years. Some people, specifically those in Asia, call it the "Dark Dragon" or, abstractly, "a lapse of time and consciousness" or a "blackout in time." Anything could be expected to happen, including an actual blackout of satellites and electricity due to major solar flares, as stated by some websites.

I don't believe that the Maya I met were completely sure what would happen either. They knew, according to the Popol Vuh, that the former creations, or humanities, perished because of their sins against the Earth and each other. Therefore, the 2012 Maya ceremonies focused on praying for forgiveness. As Don Tomás aptly stated, "All knowledge is useless if one cannot *lift one's heart*." He also said that ultimately, "humanity made it through." And some predominantly Christian circles agreed: "We have survived yet another rapture." (For a photo of Maya leader Don Tomás officiating the 2012 closing and opening of a new Maya era, see plate 2.)

3

THE INAUGURATION OF PLAZA OXLAJUJ B'AQTUN

To commemorate the New Era that dawned on December 21, 2012, Don Tomás had a plaza with elaborate sculptures specially constructed in Chichicastenango, as tradition required him to do and as the ancestral leaders had always done. In ancient times, Maya leaders had the freedom to build pyramids and grand plazas with steles. In the more recent past, however, the Maya people were persecuted and killed for expressing their culture. Don Tomás was courageous to build a Maya site for the first time since the Spanish Conquest, and the Plaza Maya, or Plaza Oxlajuj B'aqtun, is the world's only permanent site built for the purpose of celebrating this occasion.

DECEMBER 19, 2012

In a gazebo above the Plaza Oxlajuj B'aqtun, Don Tomás greeted the various representatives of the EU and ambassadors of the United States, Korea, and the Netherlands, as well as several leaders of Guatemalan politics and the industrial sector, who financed the construction of the plaza. Their presence represented the world community in this cosmic event concerning the whole planet. They all arrived, mostly by helicopter, to attend the celebrations here in the center of today's Maya experience.

The scorching sun was high in the sky when the participants began an arduous but symbolic walk from the altar room (office), through the cobblestoned streets of the town, over dirt roads, among the colorful gravestones of the cemetery, and down to the shady tent above the newly built plaza, specially prepared for the leader's guests. This journey symbolized the start of the inauguration celebration of the Plaza Oxlajuj B'aqtun.

Don Tomás gave collective and individual blessings in the Quiché language to all present. He then turned to several financiers and state representatives and ceremonially placed a Maya handwoven headscarf on their heads as a symbol of highest honor and of long-lasting friendship and commitment to the Maya.

Not all of the townspeople seemed content with the oh-so-special treatment of the foreigners and entrepreneurs. History had shown them that the White Man was a terrible oppressor, and opening up to a new chapter in time would not be a simple thing, even for the Maya people. In addition, Cementos Progreso, the most controversial—but also the most productive and financially significant—cement-producing company, had received the responsibility of sponsoring the material for the sculptures in the plaza, as they had agreed to foot the bill for the project when the Maya administration ran short of funds. This raised many eyebrows, because Cementos Progreso's facility was built on sacred Maya land, which angered some of Don Tomás's people. In fact, the sponsor plaques at the base of the sculptures strangely disappeared shortly after construction.

As I found out later in private conversation, Don Tomás had made another unpopular decision when he put a Capitoline white architect on the job instead of a Maya one. Politically, however, this was a smart move by the Maya leader, as it created foreign interest in investing in Guatemala, which initiated a flow of much-needed monetary resources into the region of El Quiché. Nevertheless, a few years later people's lack of understanding and envy revealed many hidden enemies who would cause the leader's popularity to drop.

It is important to note that, according to Don Tomás's team, the Guatemalan government agreed to promote the northern Guatemalan tropical city of Tikal as the center for welcoming the New Era to distract the expected visiting masses from descending on Chichicastenango. While archaeological sites of abandoned cities such as Tikal remain significant as ancestral sites, because it is uninhabited today, the living Maya view Tikal as an energetically dead place.* These sites no longer have any real energy because they no longer support human life, whereas in Chichicastenango today the fire never stops burning.

Anthropologists and archaeologists speculate on why the ancient Maya tended to abandon their cities. Firsthand conversations with Julio David, a Maya lawyer educated in his own tradition, can give us an explicit answer. The ancient Maya used to abandon a place when their priests had determined that it had lost its energy and would move on to build a new city in another place. "A place with energy" is a place where people live—one like Chichicastenango today where people still go about their lives, working, raising their families, and celebrating the sacred days of the year.

The coming of the New Era was celebrated in various places throughout the Central American region. Nevertheless, it was the Quichéan center of Chichicastenango where the representatives of all El Quiché departments and the heads of several other Maya districts came to celebrate.

As can be expected in every small community, some inhabitants rejected the new sacred site. They claimed it to be too removed from the center of town, which, with the ancient pyramids—though now covered by Christian churches—they consider the only main sacred ground. Of

---

*According to the Don Tomás's lawyer, Julio David Diaz Chay, in his interview with me on December 14, 2012.

course, there would have been no room to construct yet another important structure in the already overcrowded town, so the new plaza had to be built on the outskirts, which created a new, expanded center and caused the town to grow beyond its borders. The new plaza was meant to be a place for Maya and visitors alike. Tourists were being taken there during the day to get to know the plaza as a piece of Maya history and mythology. Set behind the cemetery, it was not an easy place to get to, especially during the night when some ceremonies were being conducted. Not many tourists wanted to journey through the dark, so nighttime was when the Maya were able to hold their ceremonies undisturbed by paparazzi-like photographers.

Two days before the official opening workers were still digging up ground and installing monuments in the new plaza. Witnessing this was extremely emotional. Before my eyes, a great historic moment of human civilization was unfolding, much like the Egyptian pyramids must have. The laboring workers, perspiring, dug with hand tools and sent their sounds of hammering toward the green mountains. Free of industrial noise, without machines, is how the Maya have constructed all of their pyramids and how all the ancient civilizations were built. Rather than inventing new forms of technology, the Maya build by trusting the ancient ways that originated at a time when their procreators gave them the tools for life. The Maya believe that the ancestors had a more profound insight, and therefore they value the repetition of the original information received in ancient times more highly than contemporary man's progress. Like the ancient sites from previous moments in Maya history, this place, the Plaza Oxlajuj B'aqtun, will become one of the centers of the Maya world.

Real time merged with ancient when the Maya workers placed white basalt sculptures depicting mythological figures in the center and at each of the four cardinal points of the round plaza. Contemporary and partially fictitious in style though not in content, the plaza's concept combined ancient Maya mythology with a contemporary global interpretation and signification.

IMAGERY OF THE PLAZA OXLAJUJ B'AQTUN

The imagery, directed by Don Tomás and executed by an anonymous sculptor, focused on representing the coexistence of contemporary Maya life and postcolonial civilization. The new plaza aimed to give future generations hope and a reason to be optimistic regarding the future. Manuel Xiloj, the right-hand man and scribe of Don Tomás, explained the imagery to me.

Across from the entrance, in the eastern part of the plaza, a female figure knelt in prayer with a figurative parrot perched on her head. Don Manuel explained that Don Tomás instructed the sculptor to include features representing all Maya historical dynasties, and the parrot, or *maq'uq'*, was a symbol for the dynasty of Coban. The pedestal displayed a relief depicting the encounter between a conquistador on a horse and a Maya warrior on foot. The warrior held a shield featuring the symbol of an angry sun, a sign of force and protection.

The center of the plaza harbored the main pair of figures. Their pedestals displayed scenes depicting incidences of "the first encounter of civilizations" when Europeans intruded on Maya territory. On top of the two pedestals were seated mythical figures with strict-looking masklike faces. They represented the Ancestral Grandparents, Xpiyacoc and Xmukané. The figures were placed facing in opposite directions. Grandfather Xpiyacoc faced the center of the plaza, while Grandmother Xmukané faced away from it. José Luis Tigüilá, the municipality's Maya speaker and expert on Maya culture, explained: "Xmukané is the Ancestral Grandmother of time. She symbolizes the Earth. She touches her breast, signifying that this is where we humans come from, the Earth. The breast is the symbol for nurturing, and time is at her behind." To the Maya, the "nucleus of time" is biologically and visually conceived in the human coccyx, and this is symbolically represented in the plaza statues (read more in chapter 4 under "Perceptions of Time"). (For a photo of the ancestoral sculptures in the Plaza Oxlajuj B'aqtun, see plate 3.)

Manuel Xiloj elaborated on an equally valid ecological perspective, stating that the grandmother holds her breast in concern for man's destructive treatment of planet Earth. Duality is a fundamental characteristic of Maya cosmology, and this dual sense of being can be observed in most of the elements depicted on the plaza.

Mr. Tigüilá emphasized that these ancestors and the numinous powers were not, as often portrayed in non-Maya sources, "Gods dressed in animal skin." They should rather be interpreted as elements of time. "The Maya man respects time."

The rear ends of the figures drew my attention. They depicted the sculpted abstraction of the sun in warrior-protection mode as was suggested in the shields of Maya warriors. The supposed temperature or polarity of the sun symbol was no coincidence and could be related to the South American hot-cold medicinal concept.

In the Plaza Oxlajuj B'aqtun, before the sculptures of the Ancestral Grandparents, a sculpture of a serpent was erected, standing tall in the form of a boa constrictor. Although this species of snake does not live in Central America, the sculptor perceived it as a telling depiction of the Maya serpent Kan, the snake that represents justice and rectification. Don Tomás's decision to have it placed in the center of the plaza reflects this ruler's motivation—to see justice as the center of his ruling term.

The east of the plaza displayed the sculpture of a mermaid. Facing north, she stood for the unruly energy of water and for fluidity and creativity, the Maya energy of Imox (described more in part 3).

On the west side across from the mermaid and facing south stood a male figure wearing the skin of a jaguar and a feathered tail. The image depicted a shaman-warrior. The jaguar is the guardian spirit of the shaman, and many men born under the sign of a jaguar (I'x) become an ajq'ij (shaman-priest/warrior, or daykeeper).

The exit and entrance to the mythological world depicted in the plaza lay to the west. Mr. Tigüilá described the chained lion figure placed there as the "Guardian of Time" or the "Chained World." According to him, the world has been kidnapped through contamination of the earth, the air, and the water. I assumed that this ecological explanation hid one that was more political.

In the Maya society, as in many others, too many things cannot be expressed to their fullest or even spoken out loud. It must be stated at this point that not all inhabitants, and not even all spiritual guides, approve of the iconography of the sculptures in this plaza. In 2012, there was no particular spot in the plaza for the sacred fire. As the central point of each ceremony, the fire should also be located in the center of the plaza. The Oxlajuj B'aqtun fire ceremonies, under the command of Don Tomás, were held on the southern side next to the plaza. After 2012, I observed many ajq'ijab,* including Don Juan Camajay Pinula, chief of the Ancestral Maya National Council, who led the New Year ceremony in March 2013, conducting their fire ceremonies in the center.

---

*Ajq'ijab is the plural form of ajq'ij.

4

**HONORING THE
CYCLES OF TIME,
NATURE, AND SPACE**

PERCEPTIONS OF TIME

Although Einstein discovered relativity and perceived time as events, much of Western science today relates to time as a fixed entity, as reasoned by Parmenides. The Maya concept of time can also be defined as twofold, as Absolute Time and Ordinary Time, although there may be many other layers of time to be discussed in the future. The two approaches differ, however, in a significant way. In Western science time is mostly considered a quantity rather than a quality or qualities with characteristics. To the Maya, counting time is a "key cultural pattern" (Vogt 1985, 167),* and, as is commonly known, the Ancient Maya have created numerous calendars calculating a variety of what might be called rhythms of time (details in part 3 of this book). The Maya do not count their days for the purpose of counting a number entity that has been cleaned of its substance. Time is not only moving

---

*See also Vogt's concept of "replication" (1969, 571).

but also has substance filled with life and intention. They perceive qualities of time as did ancient people living before Christianity. The Maya understand the qualities or characteristics of time as a being*— or rather beings—as living entities. What they are and how the Maya use them, much of this book will expose.

Western science, in its perception of quantitative time, might eventually edge toward a dynamic concept of time (such as the Maya have). Physicists such as Fay Dowker (2018) have started to look for a way out of the concept of fixed time. Dowker says that her teacher Stephen Hawking only touched on the question of whether time really passes. Dowker herself started to look for answers in Buddhism, where time is perceived as "becoming." If that is so, Buddhism and Maya consciousness might close the gap between time as a lifeless fixed entity and time as a process or processes. If time is in fact a process, or processes, as Dowker puts forward, I would argue that time must then be driven by intention, which would finally imply that there is mind† behind or in time. This would show time clearly as a living being, or beings. This premise of a concept of time as a living being or beings, which is supported by the Maya concept of time, will require further observation and evaluation. Nevertheless, in the light of this thought I respectfully question Einstein's famous quotation "God does not play dice" and wonder if someone does play with dice after all.

Clifford Geertz (1973, 391f) has discovered that certain Balinese calendars state time as a quality, or rather that there are different qualities for different days, which is a system comparable to that of the Maya. The Maya distinguish time as an entity of quantity and of quality. While time moves events along, each day has meaning. These events create history and destiny. Particularly, the spiritual Cholq'ij calendar gives testimony of how time is alive. Each of the twenty days of a month in this calendar is associated with a particular Maya day-energy, the so-called

---

*This is not to be confused with Parmenides's idea of static time being immobile.
†This is not to be confused with George Berkeley's (1734) concept stating that space depends on minds.

nawal and its related symbol, which exhibits that certain energy and has the power to influence humanity and the world. Each nawal can be distinguished from the others by its different qualities. Shaman-priests work with these energies and call on them on the appropriate day of the calendar or whenever they need to work with the energy of a particular day. This is very specific to Maya spirituality. Twenty days repeat within each of thirteen monthly cycles. Therefore, when the Maya count time, it is not to distinguish Monday from Tuesday but mostly to count back (or forward) to determine the specific quality of a day and its corresponding event in the past, present, or future. (More will be explained in part 3 of this book.)

In light of the concept of time as living entities as described above, it is not surprising that the Maya relate time to the human body. Mr. Tigüilá, among others, demonstrated this for me using the central sculptures in the Plaza Oxlajuj B'aqtun. Mr. Tigüilá translates the Quichéan word on the plaque at the entrance to the plaza, *b'aqtun,* into English as "coccyx." He explained that the coccyx is the very "center of Maya cosmology." Envisioning this reveals the gap between Maya and Western thinking, and possibly our inability to grasp the significance of time in its depth. While Western thought has ripped apart the understanding of time and space, the Maya see them as tied together, even considering a human being as a physical and visible microcosmos for the concept of time. The correlation between micro- and macrocosmos is real to the Maya, and the connection is reflexivity. The Maya are educated to think reflexively, while the people in the industrialized world, I would argue, need to relearn the flexibility of mind that connects the world's dimensions—perhaps by studying Comenius and/or a certain phenomenological approach.

To the Maya, the coccyx represents the very nucleus of time. In it, they see a time cycle concluding and then revolving back to its beginning, starting a new cycle thereafter. This invisible and yet visually imaginable concept teaches us how the Maya perceive the human being as a part of the cosmic movements. Humans are embedded in the universe, where they hold their place.* The coccyx, to the Maya, is a place where past and future meet to conclude creation and then create all over again. The underlying imagery reflects a biologically mirrored or integrated display of universal time. The concept has a visual correspondence to the universal macrocosmos as well as a tangible one to the biological microcosmos of a human being. In other words, time has a manifestation that is reflected in human biology. Intimately correlated, man is a part of the cosmos and its manifestation. There is no separation between nature and man. Time-space and the influencing forces within it are the structures that human life and actions depend on and are moved by. As Mercedes de la Garza would say, "Time orders history" (1975, 103), with an emphasis on "orders."

In archaeological glyphic depictions, the ancient Maya carry their ancestor in the back part of the lower body where the coccyx resides. Here, in the nucleus of time, the coccyx symbolizes the past and is simultaneously a link to the future, because humans move through time. José Luis Tigüilá says that it is where past, present, and future come together. On the forehead, they wear a symbol of their guardian spirit (nawal), which is the energy of the calendar day on which they were born. Everything depicted in a human's world has its corresponding equal in the universe. Perhaps with the Maya one might say that matter, including human beings, is made out of time.

PERCEPTIONS OF CYCLIC ORDER

The Maya respect for time depicts each person as a biological individual or member of a legacy and as an element of time cycles. A person is not only a singular or individual sequential occurrence in a historical time line but an eternal protagonist embedded and participating in recurring events in vast cycles of time as well. The fact that time cycles reoccur

---

*In Christianity, the body of Jesus Christ placed in the center of the cross represents a similar point of significance of cosmic dimension.

might indicate that the things or energies within it, including humans, reoccur as well.

Henri-Charles Puech (1958) explains all Gnostic systems of time as follows:

> Time is part of a cosmic order; on its own level it is an effect and an expression of that order. If it moves in a circle it is because, in its own way, it imitates the cyclical course of the stars on which it depends. Its endlessness, its repetition of conjunctures, are, in a mobile form, images of the unchanging, perfect order of an eternal universe, eternally regulated by fixed laws, an order of which the heavens, with the uniform revolution of their luminaries, offer still more sublime images. (43)

> The Greeks, as many pre-Christian cultures, conceived of time as above all cyclical or circular, returning perpetually upon itself, self-enclosed, under the influence of astronomical movements which command and regulate its course with necessity. For Christianity, on the contrary, time is bound up with the Creation and continuous action of God. [As opposed to the Greek view, the world of the Christians (including God) is created in time and must end in time.] (46)

> The world of the Christians . . . begins with the first chapter of Genesis and ends in the eschatological perspectives of the Apocalypse. Moreover, the Creation, the Last Judgment, and the intermediary period extending from one to the other are all unique. This created, unique world, which began, which endures, and which will end in time, is finite, limited at both extremities of its history. It is neither eternal nor infinite in its duration; it will never be repeated, nor will the events that occur in it. The world is wholly immersed in time. (46)

It is needless to point out that humanity has had many definitions of freedom, but none of them was lived eternally so far, which left the human being "free" only in a temporary time and space. Puech describes the Greek perception of time as cyclical, Christian time as unilinear, and Gnostic time as a broken line that shatters other perceptions into bits.

A straight line, as Puech elaborates (1958, 42), cannot detect or follow any rhythm. It kills the natural rhythms that time experiences.* The consequences of thinking of time as flowing in a straight line are grave. It makes people think in straight lines entirely, gets them to build cities in gridlocks of uncreative curvelessness, and makes them less attuned and adaptable to "curvy" nature. Naturally, a few generations of this kind of thinking leads people into a technocratic existence, unable to live in nature and tending to ignore, damage, or destroy it, as evidenced by the actions of modern Western culture.

The Maya acknowledge a time-space determined by the sun in which earthly life is possible. However, they observe time over periods that reach beyond one individual's lifetime. Their astronomers have been doing so without interruption since the ancient past. Through observational astronomy the Maya could also calculate time-space mathematically. Through observational astronomy they have been able to record vast amounts of time and to grasp their cycles.

I believe that Western societies fail to grant themselves the opportunity to try to understand time as stretching over generations within vast cycles consisting of thousands of generations. It is therefore logical to assume that within their fairly short historic perceptions and their interpretation, manipulated conveniently to support the (selfish) interests of each nation, the Western approach may be unable to achieve more than their vision of linear time cycles allows. Our focus on linear history makes us unable to even attempt to see a thing in its organic totality. One could say that by emphasizing our individualism, we live life in a desperate way. We remain unaware of our ability to connect to past and future generations to achieve a subsequent integration into wholeness.

---

* . . . and that the Maya count in the measure of nawales.

We may assign special significance to the manner in which the Maya perceive the cycle of life differently from contemporary Westerners. Despite the fact that Christian belief holds that there is an afterlife, in the Western worldview all things have a beginning and an end—in that order. To the Maya things end and then begin anew, and they think in that order. Their day begins close after midnight and takes a turn downward after 12:00 p.m., correlating to the sun's movement. Spiritual ceremonies therefore begin in the early morning hours.

Christianity flourished when rationality was imposed, and so church leaders desperately wanted to break the Greek cycle of time. History does repeat itself, and this process can be witnessed. The Greeks eventually gave in to one way of thinking rather than continuing to allow multiple ways. Giving up on a good part of their reality, they limited their beliefs to one religion, standardized their laws, and adopted one calendar. The Western cultures that developed soon after the epoch of ancient Greece tried to globalize culture and language first into Latin and later into English. Instead of being open to the concept of cycles of time and different ways of thinking, these cultures thrived on being right by imposing rational ideas, including their singular way of expression—the written word. I wonder, aren't we, the Westerners, the illiterates of the world?

Beginning in ancient Greece and Rome, the process of some of the world's conversion to Christianity became stronger, more accepted, and little by little imposed a hierarchic or linear time concept. Church leaders convinced people that the way to free themselves from the never-ending cycles of life was to be catapulted beyond them into an abstract though individualized eternal afterlife in which they would live close to perfection (God). Subsequently, this shift in perception pressed time into a scheme that caused all things to move from a beginning to an end. Leaving the historic-philosophical perspective for a moment and turning to the non-Western world of the Maya, the end in their cyclic cosmology is never truly an end, because it is always followed by a new beginning. Consequently, time, and with it human consciousness, are endless.

Puech reminds us that for the Greeks, as it is for the Maya, there was no absolute chronological "before" and "after" (1958, 42).

No point in a circle is a beginning or middle or end in the absolute sense; or else all points are these indifferently. The starting point to which the "apocatastasis" or the completion of the "Great Year" restores the course of things in a movement which is regression as well as progression is never anything but relative. (41)

Finally, Puech's illustration of movement can reflect how the Maya are able to predict the past and future.* To them, because everything cycles back to its point in time, real change is illusory. Past, present, and future are the same thing in their conception of an unchanged universe. As they see it, as long as things remain the same, the future will be the same. That is the concept by which the Maya have always lived, and in that concept lies the reason why traditionalists such as the Maya leader Don Tomás and the Elders of the Quiché attempt to keep their society homogenous, and also why they tend to do things exactly as their forefathers did. For in doing so, they can predict some of the future, living by the mantra that was also known by our European ancestors: "He who knows his past, also knows his future."

I would consider the above to be one of the main Maya teachings to people of industrialized societies who, on the other end of the spectrum, tend to run away from themselves and who they really are, constantly changing their lifestyles and calling their changes progress.

As with the predecessors of any preindustrial society, the Maya method is one of consciously integrating (fitting) into nature. Through a dynamic oral tradition between the generations, large and old parts of history have remained active in Maya consciousness. This way of bridging time is the secret to the survival of their culture. From this perception of time, the Maya experience of life, the world, nature, the

---

*As revealed to me in personal conversation with members of the Maya administration.

cosmos, and divinity is not separated. It is an integrated one—one that phenomenologists like Jan Patočka call "natural." (See the introduction to this book.)

From this perspective, we can grasp the Maya need and responsibility to respect all of those components of life, and we can see why modern societies have lost so much. We can also understand why, to contemporary Westerners who have lost their sense of cyclical time, it makes sense to incorporate the afterlife into each person's existence. However, to the Maya the afterlife is not something beyond or dead or ended; it is continuous, encompassing every moment.

Time being tied to the bodily experience furthermore enables the skilled Maya shaman to overpass time-space borders and travel in time and space. The problem of physicality in Western philosophy does not arise for the Maya, since they are aware of a nonphysical being within the human body that can change time and space by leaving the material body.

PERCEPTIONS OF SPACE

The Maya concept of time and space has the potential to contribute greatly to Western studies of the consciousness of time and space, though to understand the Maya concept of time and space requires a shift in perspective. Much has been written about sacred space.* The Popol Vuh describes the creation of the world as "halving the cord, stretching the cord, in the sky, on the earth, the four sides, the four corners" (D. Tedlock 1996, 63). This becomes a human's living space, both sacred and profane. It is a time-space created by the sun and defined by the equinoxes and solstices. The time the sun takes to go from one corner of the world to another, and the space it shines its light on, is the time-space that humans can occupy and where they can breathe and

---

*Some of the more significant works were written by Mircea Eliade (1991, 2012) and Victor Turner (1969).

see and grow. Where there is no light, there is no human life. (See the description of the Palo Volador in chapter 5.)

It seems obvious that from their location on Earth, in Central America, the Maya are far removed from the North and South Poles. Therefore, the daily east-west movement of the sun may be more prominent in their thinking, because it effects them more than the sun's seasonal north-south movements. Nevertheless, they are aware of north and south of course, and the act of giving respect to all four directions is instrumental in all prayers.

The Maya do, however, also recognize space outside of the space currently inhabited by earthly living entities. One that I know of in Quiché is called *najt,* which is space-time plus frequency (Barrios 2009, 89). It is the space from which everything was created. Phonetically, this word sounds similar to the German word for "night," *Nacht;* their common origin would be important to study in the future.

One Maya cosmic space is our galaxy. Its Center, the galaxy's zenith, they call "Heart of Sky." It is the most important instance (authority) in Maya cosmology and was the point of attention of the 2012 cosmic event. All prayers begin by calling on "Heart of Sky." Its centrality rules Maya thought and action. Our planet, located on the Orion arm about two-thirds the distance from the center of the galactic spiral, moves around this center, allowing the Maya to recognize time as cyclic, as explained above.

Based on Aristotle, who explained embodied space as the structure where body can act, we see the perspective of how the individual body experiences space. This individualized conception of space also correlates to George Berkeley's (1734) concept of time, which states that time depends on individual minds. If space—and time—depend on the individual, then both can also be altered by the individual, an argument that correlates with the Maya experience in which shaman-priests manipulate events in time and space. The method for doing so mostly occurs by manipulating fire, the main element of communication with the numinous beings. The shaman-priest puts his intention into the fire by speaking to it. The intention reaches his powerful numinous helpers with whom he communicates and convinces to change an event. This is how prayer works too.

As for manipulating space, Einstein proved that time and space can be bent. Manuel Xiloj provided an analogy: the expansion of space is analogous to what happens when light hits a drop of water and opens it up, providing a view or vision of the space inside. By this, a new space opens.

The Maya view of time and space is greatly expanded compared to the Western view. We can grasp the idea of shifting space, for example, when illustrating the world's map from a non-Eurocentric view, placing China or Africa in the center of the map. That alone, for a Westerner, is hard for the habit of the mind. Applying this to time, placing a difference in beginning and end, could enable Western civilization to experience a completely different and more compassionate perspective on the world.

The memorial plaque at the Plaza Oxlajuj B'aqtun aptly portrays the Maya world at the axis of the world's civilizations by referring to "one people's world." This statement, which sets the Maya in the world's center globally, may seem ethnocentric from the Maya perspective. But it is important to realize that to the ancient Maya, other civilizations were not rationally known or didn't matter to their world. As every center of the ancient world, an axis connects to heaven and brings down cosmic energy. It is therefore that a place of energy is a center (compare Eliade 1991, 12–13). Even to the contemporary Maya their main world is their culture and territory, though some confusion arises due to global living. Each culture's worldview focuses on itself for the sake of maintaining unity, although globalization has extended this concept in our contemporary time frame. We are currently expanding the cultural vocabulary that would again unify this new, globally interconnected frame. What once was served by world religions needs a new frame today. To the Maya, human existence lies on the axis between the two cosmic focal points: "Heart of Sky" and "Heart of Earth." To them it is the responsibility of human beings to hold together the connection between Sky and Earth for cosmic harmony, which can be achieved through the good behavior of humanity. Little did I know at the time how my own future would collide with these ancient teachings and that I, too, would become responsible for helping to hold together this cosmic connection.

5

TRADITIONAL
REENACTMENTS DURING
THE SOLSTICE SEASON

Festivities are moments of regeneration. In particular, cultures based on ritual calendrical systems cherish festivities as a time out of the ordinary. They serve to connect ordinary with mythical time and keep a channel open for understanding various levels of time. In secular societies festivities are excessive. They involve a lot of alcohol, promiscuity, violence, and, in Latin America, the dance between life and death can border on the latter or send a person beyond. It is a time of danger. Spiritual festivities, such as the one described below, attempt to create a strong sense of place and a time of purity by practicing the exact repetition of tradition or protocol. Festivities purify and are a time to let go of the ordinary and become refreshed, renewed, and revitalized.

TRADITIONAL DANCES

December 21, the day of the winter solstice, is lavishly celebrated in Chichicastenango each year in honor of the patron Santo Tomás.

The year 2012 was extraordinary for a variety of reasons, and the regular protocol was enhanced by the celebrations for the New Era. At different places throughout town, between December 8th and 22nd, dancers performed the Baile del Torito and the popular Baile de los Convite. On December 20th and 21st, the mythical-historical Baile de los Conquistadores was staged in the central plaza. The dancers are volunteers dedicating their time away from daily breadwinning to gain expertise and engage in the ritual as a personal and communal sacral service.

To participate in the drama, strict preparation is required. For one, for certain dances, dancers have to undergo a month's-long training with rehearsals, which are invitation only to family and friends. During that time, they learn the steps and, equally important, have the time to identify with the mythical role they dance.

The men and women embodying a mythical figure have to fast for five days prior to dancing.* The dancing, which lasts from morning until late at night for at least the five days of the celebrations, is performed with little rest and food. Everybody comes to see them.

The dance aims to reenact epic history and help the people come to terms with the conquerors' vision for the New World, which became the local peoples' trauma. Simultaneously it demonstrates cosmic occurrences. In the dance, the splendidly dressed and decorated dancers represent the sixteenth-century conquistadors and the Quichéan warriors with their heroic leader Tecún Umán. They are attired in masks all made in studios in Chichicastenango, in abstracted sixteenth-century European fashion. Their masks mimic white-skinned and blue-eyed men and women. (For a photo of the Baile de los Conquistadores, see plate 4.)

In attire, practice, and significance, many of the dances combine the richness of a spirituality-driven tradition of diverse cultures. Maya design, together with European and Arab customs brought in

---

*These dances are significant reenactments of an arche (from the Greek word archē, meaning "origin"), which is a sequence of events of mythical substance (Huebner 1985, 135) that is reenacted with the same significance each time it is repeated.

by the Spaniards, are all represented in the costumes. In the Western Highlands those traditions are cherished and kept alive so as to remember and to strengthen the identity of the community.

Each dance tells a different story, and many respond to the population's need to adapt to the changes resulting from the Conquest as well as today's cultural infiltration from Western societies. A future fact-check will show what recent globalization contributed to many societies respecting tradition, not only the Maya.

Some dances originated in the Classic Period of Maya civilization (250–900 CE). Along with certain historical events, the dancers reenact the arche, the primordial event with its Maya worldview. In this event, God, or another sacred being, has instructed the first people and given them extraordinary powers. To keep these powers alive over time, the event is passed down through this enacted and oral tradition. History and mythos are combined in each dance and preserve a unifying oneness and diversity.

THE PALO VOLADOR

The Palo Volador is performed in the town center on a daily basis during the winter solstice festivities. On the eighteenth of December, a high pole is erected that is made from a tree chosen by the initiated men beforehand and cut amid ritual prayers. Its placement in the town center represents the axis of the world. Around it, two or four men fly, usually hanging upside down from long ropes bound to their ankles on one end and to the pole on the other. (For a photo of the Palo Volador, see plate 5.)

Depending on the number of flying men, a third or fifth man* sits atop the pole, high above the crowd. As time slowly unravels, he whistles sacred melodies, hoping to evoke the sun's energy with his breath

---

*The number of men participating seems to be more a question of economy rather than a question of tradition. Participation may depend on availability of money and volunteers.

while harmonizing his heart with his drum and flute. The simple, flute-like sounds of his wooden chirimia* support the sentiment of flight as the men circle birdlike through the air.

Each flying man rotates 13 times, so that the four of them count 52 rotations. The ritual represents the unraveling of time, and the men, by climbing the tree into the Sky and rotating back to Earth, connect the Earth and Sky, harmonizing them in the process.

The Palo Volador mimics the creation of the world. It calls for harmonization and fertility. The enactment reflects the Popol Vuh, which describes the creation of the four-corner Sky-Earth (the world) as a long performance of

> the fourfold siding, fourfold cornering,
> measuring, fourfold staking,
> halving the cord, stretching the cord
> in the sky, on the earth,
> the four sides, the four corners,
> as it is said . . . (D. Tedlock 1996, 63–64)

The passage describes the measuring of the world. The flying men of the Palo Volador represent the four corners of the world. Together with the fifth man, the ritual forms a quincunx—a five-pointed geometrical system of spiritual value. Taking a Christian cross and projecting it into the three-dimensional, it equally consists of five such points—four forming the cross and the fifth at its heart, accentuated by the heart of Christ, possibly ascending upward.

In his dissertation, "The Shapes of Sacred Space," Christopher Powell doesn't seem to mention the Palo Volador, a ritual enacted at every important festive occasion. However, he examined the geometric shaping of sacred space by the Maya as learned from their art, artifacts, and

---

*A simple instrument cut from wood and brought by the Spaniards in the sixteenth century, probably of Arabic origin.

architecture. In it, he describes another ritual enacted by contemporary Maya in the Yucatán peninsula of Mexico—the Cha Chac ceremony.

> . . . displays geometrical constructions that are remarkably similar to those described by Landa and Duran. In this ceremony, four large posts are erected in the form of a square. . . . Placed at the center of this square is a smaller square (or double square) altar, consisting of a table with four legs. Cords or ropes are attached diagonally along the ground from the four legs of the altar to the four larger corner posts. At the four corners of the central altar stand four vertical posts. Two arched boughs are attached diagonally to the tops of each post, crossing at the upper center of the altar. At the center of this elaborate quincunx, on top of the altar and beneath the arched boughs (representing the sky and possibly the ecliptic), food and other offerings are laid. This becomes the focus of the ceremony conducted by a shaman, the purpose of which is to bring forth rain. Sometimes young boys are tied by their ankles to the four corners of the altar, and they imitate the croaking of frogs to help bring on the rain. (2010, 35)

In all the ceremonies that I have attended in El Quiché over the years I have never witnessed, as Powell describes on page 34 of his dissertation, the act of measuring space at the beginning of a ceremony. It is not exclusive to the Yucatán region though, because for the Palo Volador the ropes are measured to the length that ensures 13 cycles around the tree. A rope, possibly of a certain specific length, was definitely a part of the 2012 ritual of Tzijolaj coming down to Earth, which I describe in the following section.

WELCOMING THE NEW ERA

As I entered the crowded altar room, the dancer with the Tzijolaj wooden rider figure on his arm rounded the space in a three-step back-

and-forth rhythm. Sweat dripped from his forehead as he danced for hours and days, impersonating the sacred man. But instead of dropping from exhaustion, he later told me, he is filled with energy every time, swirling like a perpetuum mobile. (For a photo of a dancer and the Tzijolaj icon, see plate 6.)

I knelt before the cross that hangs on the front wall above the Elders who stood behind the long altar table. I usually stayed somewhere to the side unless told to do otherwise. I was the only part of the group that did not have a specific place in the scenario. I felt like the yin to the yang, like the single red bead in a determined pattern in an Indian bracelet.

To the Maya authorities I was not an anthropologist but rather more of a young woman with an open heart that brought some change to their protocol. Don Tomás said to me, "We need your heart," and I knew he didn't mean to sacrifice it. He called me "the girl with hair the color of maize." Gradually, I became a person to trust . . . and to many I became a friend.

By midday, Chichicastenango was inundated with smoke from the incense that had been burning all morning. A procession of red and green feather- and flower-decorated floats came parading through the streets. At this point, male citizens carried images of the local saints on their shoulders as they walked toward the church, accompanied by a crowd of men and women dressed in vibrant traditional attire. (For a photo of the procession, see plate 7.)

The people gazed up at the main patron saints—Santo Tomás, San José, and San Sebastian. The icons had been placed in the church the night before for safekeeping, and people had come to offer prayer and money. That morning, the icons were taken around the streets to the music of the chirimia, drums, and marimba. They were then placed on the outside steps in front of the main entrance of the biggest church, facing west toward the Calvary church.

In the meantime, in 2012, another large crowd was packed around the ceremonial fire under the steps of the Calvary church. These steps, as mentioned previously, are to the Maya the actual ancestral altar. They are often a former pyramid, purposely used by the Spanish Christians as a foundation to erect their churches. A pyramid has a base of four sides that connect at an apex. It makes sense that the Maya would revere this shape when we keep in mind the quincunx, which is the five-pointed geometrical space that forms the Maya world resembling the cosmic space relevant to humans, with its four sides and Center (the sun or the zenith). (Compare pages 45 and 50.)

Don Tomás, who had been blessing visitors on the "pyramid's" platform atop the stairs, now descended—ritually—to the large fire pit before the stairs, which was surrounded by the crowd. This descent would be mirrored a short while later by the central most important act of this event: the descent of the wise grandfather Tzijolaj, also called Santiago, that would occur in front of the main church on the eastern side of the plaza.

The leader's guests followed him in a snakelike line moving slowly and circling from right to left. Though there is not always a fire at this celebration, 2012 was a special year. Don Tomás and his followers circled several times around the large ceremonial fire, which the ajq'ijab had been kindling for some time. Like a sacral king, Don Tomás also signified with his act the lineage of all historic ancestral leaders who had led their people since primordial times. Cosmology and history go hand in hand.

As I had a somewhat liberal "joker" position, I stayed atop the platform to take photos. Many Maya and visitors alike had brought their cameras as well to capture this unique moment for eternity. (To see a photo of Don Tomás and his national and international guests with their hands together as a sign of peace, refer to plate 8.)

Don Tomás led the procession back up the pyramid, where he received the ajq'ijab. The men came up from the fire they were kindling to kneel before him and tell him what messages they had received from the flames. The fire was the primary element that enlivened the scene spiritually. It animated and stimulated the numinous powers to get in touch, protect, and speak in some form to the participants, mainly the ajq'ijab, whose blood was moved in certain body parts, which indicated how they should interpret the transmitted information.

At 12:02 p.m. on December 21, 2012, the long-expected planetary alignment occurred. Time took a breath. Don Tomás got up from his seat and positioned himself in front of the high steps of the Calvary church. Slowly the sun started to appear in the oriel window on top of the Santo Tomás church across the plaza. Everything happened so perfectly it seemed that, when the Christian church was built, capturing the solstice was taken into account.

Between the churches lay the sacred ritual space and in it hundreds of people took on their symbolic function of activating life. Their role would be forever written into Maya history by their participation as ritual dancers, float carriers, hired musicians, operators of pyrotechnics, and spectators from near and far. They, along with the group of national and international honorable guests on top of the pyramid, the leader, the ajq'ijab, the Elders, and the town and district authorities with their families, all now looked out at the major sun spectacle occurring above the main church.

High up in the Santo Tomás church window two men pulled on the ropes with all their might to ring the iron bells. At that moment, Manuel Xiloj handed Don Tomás the microphone to bid the old Oxlajuj B'aqtun farewell and welcome the new 5,125-year cycle and new 26,000-year Aq'ab'al era, the era of the sunrise. Standing high above his people, the leader delivered an elaborate speech about love and peace, translated by Don Manuel into three foreign languages.

The leader's words, symbolically coming from high above, cut through the crowded plaza and the different sound sources—the marimba band, ritual drums, chirping autochthonous flutes, and the nearly unbearable noise of firecrackers going up into the air right beside everyone.

The noise, a typical feature of every celebration, seemed necessary to draw the attention of the numinous powers and the aligning planets in particular, and to get people to cherish them, as the Book of Council requires. Despite all of this distraction, the leader's words sounded like they were coming from the gods. That evening, there, on the western side, the sun would go down anew, and the old b'aqtun would be let go.

At Santo Tomás church, a fire was lit high up in the bell tower. There we witnessed the sun rising through midday and actively taking part in the alignment of the planets. Here and now, the new b'aqtun was beginning—and with it a whole new era whose dimension we were hardly capable of grasping.

Following that, we (the administration and guests) descended the pyramid and walked through the masses of people toward the main church. There the rotating flying men of the Palo Volador defined space by moving the cords around the world tree. Flying through the air, they symbolically drew the four spatial segments that the sun travels between the solstices and equinoxes. That, in Maya cosmology, is the space that man inhabits. The fifth man represented the Center, the sun. We watched as into this sacred world-space the wooden figure of the Tzijolaj rider descended on a rope from the bell tower above. Moving slowly over the people and toward the Palo Volador, he carried a globe fitting his size and fashioned from straw that brought new life to the already established space. His descent symbolizes the sun turning the corner on December 21 of each year, but his descent had heightened significance in 2012 as the alignment took place before Heart of Sky. The old world of the Thirteenth B'aqtun ended, and before our eyes a new world introduced itself. (For a photo of the Tzijolaj rider descending, see plate 9.)

The cords reminded everyone of the primordial event told of in the Popol Vuh in which the world was created by measuring and folding space. I looked forward to the day when scientists would break through the mystery of space and discover their own way to manipulate it to create new worlds, as the ancient Maya have been doing in a way still unimagined by Westerners.

The wooden icon of the rider on his horse represented a person who, in the sixteenth century, is believed to have come with the Spaniards to the Americas. Tzijolaj, also called Santiago, had been made immortal by the reinterpretation of the day's Maya rituals. He had become the most important sacred force in El Quiché. People saw him coming as the wind element and believed that he brought prosperity to Earth. He was to spark new life and represented abundance, as was symbolized by the coins that covered the Tzijolaj figure. Later that night the dancers would move the figure around the ceremonial fire.

What to an outsider might appear as theater is a necessary means of salvation for those who grew up in the Maya culture, in the same way that the sacraments of world religions are for members of those belief structures. When following the protocol and trusting that God is doing the rest behind the scenes, miraculous things can happen. What the Greeks called mysterion, and the Catholic church calls sacramental economy, to some of us would be a wonder. For the Maya, by fostering imagination, the unimaginable can become reality. This may be hard to imagine for people who see the world as composed of many "dead" things. In the Western world many ideas or concepts are unanimated or became fixed. To the Maya, everything existing is animated and living and therefore moving, changing, and transforming. Maybe because they recognize that everything is in flux they do not need to provoke change. Vice versa, perhaps man in the industrialized world, who fixed every-thing to be secure and in control, escapes his self-inflicted system by creating change. Because their minds have been kept flexible in certain ways, the Maya can imagine and allow even space and time to expand (see the previous chapter). It is not just that they believe time and space can expand. Believing is often passive, and believing and imagining are two different things. Imagining creates an animate reality. The Maya nourish this animate reality through action and tradition.

With Santiago's coming down to Earth, the event had culminated and was winding down. We walked through town to the Hotel Santo Tomás, where Don Tomás and the municipality invited us to a lavish lunch. Later that night, we met in the altar room and walked down to the Plaza Oxlajuj B'aqtun for the night ceremony at 12:30 a.m.

Our group of about sixty people circled the plaza, knelt before the ancestral sculptures, and bestowed honor on the energies present. The spiritual guides lit the ceremonial fire at the east side of the plaza and kindled it for hours. (For a photo of the fire ceremony, see plate 10.)

Three men and one woman threw *pom* and other incense and emptied thirteen bottles of rum into the flames—thirteen corresponded to the galactic number of the Thirteenth B'aqtun. With their sacrifices and prayers, the shaman-priests managed to spark the ancestors' spirits, who appeared in the flames and spoke to them about the future. What was revealed by the morning, commoners will never know for certain. But Don Tomás, tired after the five days of continual responsibility, told me at 8:00 a.m. after the fire had wound down, that he was content. From the message the ajq'ijab had brought to him and from what he saw in the fires, he knew that Ahau was pleased. Pleasing God and the numinous powers between the cosmos and Earth is the prime responsibility of human beings, and it seems that the citizens of Chichicastenango had done it right.

Don Tomás summarized the festivities: "We had wind and rain. The fire did not go out even though it rained. That gives me hope and trust that the future will be a good one."

PART 2

DIARY OF LIFE
WITH THE MAYA

6

A FUSION OF IDEAS

December 18, 2014

In March 2013, I returned to Chichicastenango for the Maya New Year. I stayed about two months this time accompanying Don Tomás and his team on official endeavors in town, the region, and the capital. I was sent to political encounters with the UN representative for the Maya people and visited the president of the Ancestral Maya National Council north of Chichicastenango, as well as various small communities, when I was invited by their Maya mayor. I interacted with ajq'ijab and other people and learned about spirituality, medicine, and daily life. It was also the time when Easter is celebrated, and in Chichicastenango, as in other places, the Christian occasion is merged into Maya belief and honored with processions, fire ceremonies, and feasts. When I got tired of being looked at, talked to, and questioned, I took some days off and visited friends in Antigua, where I had lived many years before.

Many months later, in December 2014, once again the multicolored chicken bus carried me from Antigua to Chichicastenango, a place that to me, along with Europe and New York, had become home.

As we slowly ascended over the shoulders of the volcanos and into the green mountains, I was rocked into a state of semiconsciousness. We passed by micro villages consisting of a few houses with tin roofs that

54

were built mostly from earth or cement, the inexpensive building materials of the poor and earthquake-stricken mountain population.

One may wonder how these people manage to stay in touch with "the world." To provide an answer to that, one has to note that these people have many ways to travel—physically and spiritually. The men, women, and children in the streets were from the same culture as those who sat with me on the bus, squeezed into their seats, mostly quiet. Some of them looked curiously at me, the white woman who had taken a sudden dive into their everyday world. When traveling, I always converse with whoever is sitting next to me about their life, and they give me a glimpse into their world, simultaneously ancient and modern; theirs is a culture where time may well be eternal. Their times and spaces are not simply routine and monotonous. Instead, they are lived out much more diversely than a stranger, caught within his own native worldview, may grasp. With this book, I will try to lift a curtain so that you can have a glimpse into the rich culture I have experienced over the years.

After three hours on that bumpy road I arrived in Chichicastenango, the administrative town of the Maya Quiché, where I have friends in the Maya leadership and with many of its people. The Quichéan people are the largest ethnic group in Guatemala, and their district is called El Quiché. The citizens of Santo Tomás Chichicastenango call themselves "Masheños" after their patron Santo Tomás. As with many things there, the town has several names. In addition to Chuwilá, the locals call it Swan Tinamit—the "City between Ravines."

Shaken up from the ride, I fell out of the rattling bus and went directly to my friend's office, which was also called Swan Tinamit, and was a center where young Maya teachers receive training in their own culture, a privilege they were deprived of during the forty years of guerrilla warfare. Its CEO is José Luis Tigüilá. Dressed in Western clothes, he is a rather atypical sight in Chichicastenango, where most men and women dress in traditional Maya attire, but he is a steady man with a deep voice and strong principles.

I described my first encounter with José Luis in part 1. Since then he had taught me much about Maya understanding and how to read the Maya glyphs. I was his guest at his formative training sessions for Maya teachers, which left my anthropologic education from Western universities far behind and gave me insight into Maya thinking. (For a photo of José Luis Tigüilá, see plate 11.)

José Luis Tigüilá is a gifted teacher. Many Maya students have profited from his eloquence and ability to communicate Maya knowledge. With these skills he is predestined for his position of "First Spokesman of the Maya Administration." He also wrote the foreword to this book. He explained some fundamental factors of Maya glyphic writing. First, the Maya read from bottom up. Mr. Tigüilá gives a logical explanation: "Everything grows from the ground up." More importantly for Maya epigraphy, all writing is based on what the shaman-priests have received through the numinous powers in fire ceremonies or dreams, and the same key should be used to decipher the information.

After my chat with José Luis, I loaded my luggage into a tuk-tuk, a three-wheeled taxi, and went to my friend Josefa Xiloj's house in a nearby neighborhood. Her new household help was expecting me and gave me a warm welcome. Josefa is the sister of Manuel Xiloj, and I met her at the Plaza Oxlajuj B'aqtun inauguration in December 2012. Josefa works as the director of a financial cooperative that José Luis leads. Ever since I saw her for the first time at the inauguration, she has felt very dear to my heart. There was an instant bond, as if I had known her for a long, long time. Her long black hair, Maya attire, intellect, and female tenderness make this woman a beauty, inside and out. She must be about forty-eight years old, but nobody knows her real age or her birthday—not even her. (For a photo of Josefa and me in 2015, see plate 12.)

I was lucky that Josefa had invited me to stay with her during such a busy and festive time of the year. If I had stayed in one of the few hotels in the town center, as I had in previous years, I would have had to contend with fireworks and music until 3:00 a.m., when the community begins the day with ritual dances and much more. In 2012 when I participated in all the festivities, I hardly got any sleep, either because I had been up for the activities before sunrise or because I was at the fire ceremonies until 1:00 a.m.

Over delicious chunks of cooked root vegetables, carrots, and *güisquil,* Josefa and I got caught up on the events and experiences that had happened since I had left town in spring 2013, a year and a half earlier. Josefa had to return to the office, and I was excited about ascending to the town center to merge and mingle with the buzz of the solstice and Christmas season.

It was December 18, and the festivities of the winter solstice were already in full swing. They accelerate as the days go by, beginning on December 3 through December 12 when the Holy Mary is honored. They reach a culmination with the solstice on December 21 and extend into December 23. From there, events slowly subside into the Christmas celebrations.

🪶

The Maya tradition, like all nonsecularized cultures, celebrates the winter solstice. However, because of the persecution during the Spanish Inquisition in the sixteenth century and Western dominion ever since, the Christian tradition was blended with the original belief system, and what emerged was an amazingly rich syncretism. Make no mistake, the Maya culture and religion have undergone many changes. In many parts of the country this religious symbiosis and mimicry remains essential for survival even today, ideologically as well as physically. To penetrate and disentangle the Maya elements based on cosmic events from the linear-hierarchic Christian ones may be an anthropological goal that cannot be reached without experiencing the lifelong journey of Maya spirituality.

As described in the previous chapter, December 18 marks the beginning of the daily performed Palo Volador during which men in monkey costumes fly hanging upside down from long ropes that are bound to each man's ankle on one end and to a pole on the other. The fifth man, sitting atop the pole, represents the connection to the sun, and his song may be considered to be the song of the world.

The Palo Volador ritual's mythical and cosmological narratives go back to mythology and events described in the Popol Vuh. As with the earlier described cosmic meaning of the ritual, the historic-turned-mythical event it re-creates has never been written down (as far as we know). It has, however, been orally put in stone, so to speak, by its retelling and reenactment over and over throughout time, passing on from one generation to the next.

Like many Maya traditions, the Palo Volador is a fusion of many ideas. In addition to representing the creation of the world, the unraveling of time, and the harmonization of Earth, Sky, and Center, the Palo Volador is also connected to another story. The narrative goes that the Santo Tomás icon had been found in the woods, and several men were assigned to guard it overnight. When I asked, nobody was able to give me a concrete historic time of this event, other than that it may have occurred when the Quichéans escaped to Chuwilá (Chichicastenango) from the former capital of Q'umarkaj (near Santa Cruz del Quiché) when it was occupied by the Spaniards. The icon's guards, the story continues, fell asleep, and the icon was stolen. As a punishment for their failure, the guards were transformed into monkeys. Ever since that day they have been living in the trees as mediators between the upper numinous beings and humanity, eternalized in the Palo Volador ritual. Obviously, this is not really a punishment per se, as Maya law does not punish but uses social pressure and education instead. The syncretism in this myth is evident; one can hardly recognize the original ancient cosmic event in this mix of story.

But the Palo Volador's symbolism does not end there. The twenty energies or days of the Cholq'ij calendar possess various appearances according to their characteristics. Since certain animals have energies that correspond to these day signs, or nawales, glyphic writing uses animal pictures to express those energies. The monkey is the animal appearance of B'atz'—the first of these twenty energies. B'atz' also appears as a rope. In the Palo Volador ritual, B'atz' takes on its alternative form of a rope and, as such, embodies the energy that unravels time. The ritual, and with it the men's slow rotation around the pole, portrays this unraveling and serves to rejuvenate and harmonize the energies of the world.

This ritual symbolizes the unraveling of time. As we saw in part 1, time plays a much more complex and real-life role in the Maya worldview than in industrial societies, where it has been limited to living by the clock only. The Maya regard time as in pre-Christian times, very much in a Platonic way. Plato, as elaborated on by Henri-Charles Puech defined time for all Gnostic systems as follows:

> That which is determined and measured by the revolution of the celestial spheres is the mobile image of immobile eternity which it imitates by moving in a circle; consequently both the entire cosmic process and the time of our world of generation and decay develop in a circle or according to an indefinite succession of cycles, in the course of which the same reality is made, unmade, and remade, in conformity with an immutable law and determinate alterations. (1958, 38).

Each historic epoch has its distinct worldview, and sometimes it is necessary to return to a concept of thought from two thousand years ago to be able to understand a people who share the world with us in a different geographical location or, in a globalized society, at the office desk next to ours.

Returning to the cyclical Greek conception of time not only helps to mentally remove oneself from one's habitual thought matrix and understand the Maya and other cultures, it also reveals our own ancestors' foundation of thought—European or other. Much confusion has come with the Gregorian calendar, which, since 1582, substitutes the nearly equal Julian calendar. With this time system, fairly new in human history, Christian festivities do not match influential celestial events any longer. Christmas, Easter, and New Year's stopped corresponding to the natural cosmic order. Man, or rather the church, has taken over and set up an artificial system that has derailed more than half of the world's population into a state of being off the universal reality. For now, we struggle to understand the Maya. In the same way, not long ago, it was unimaginable to coexist with the Chinese in the correlated way we do today, let alone accept and understand their lunar calendar. Today, its coexistence is on the map.

✑

When I got to the church plaza in the afternoon, the flying had already begun. The initiated men climb the tree several times a day until the rounds that correspond to the 360 days of the particular calendar have been flown.

I watched the *voladores* for a while and then strolled through the market. Once a beautiful site of little houses with tiled roofs, as Josefa's mother remembered it, the market had not always been neglected. The market used to be integrated into the town. Today, it is gradually taking over more and more space, cramming the rest of the town together.

Many people come from the surrounding villages, in need or out of greed, insisting on their right to market their products at this lucrative place. They haul their goods in their cars to the market, setting up their plastic tarpaulins early in the morning. Some don't have cars so they walk there, carrying their products on their backs. Others travel on buses. The market is overcrowded, but the administration struggles to put a hold on the people from out of town who claim their right to participate. Fines don't work very well in Chichicastenango. When they were used in the past to control who had the right to sell and who did not, there were incidents of rioting and stalls and buildings were burned down.

Don Tomás came walking down the crowded main market street, heading for the nearby Santo Tomás church. His traditional Maya attire differed slightly from that of the rest of the men. The embroidered red sun in the center of his solar plexus distinguished him as Guatemala's

Maya leader. The attire of the other members of the administration and the ajq'ijab depicts the snakelike lines symbolizing the vital telluric energies between Sky and Earth and with it man's blood flow. A thick head scarf, called a *sut,* covers their heads and distinguishes them as sacred, or at least honorable.

Don Tomás's face lit up as he spotted me in the crowd. I respectfully kissed his hand because we were in public, but he pulled me to his heart and hugged me like a father and a friend, and that is what he feels like to me. We exchanged a few quick words, as much as my lack of Quichéan language allowed. Besides the talking, we exchanged "much heart." He was with his ten-year-old daughter, Mariza, a sweet, intelligent-looking girl with spiritual eyes.

Don Tomás told me to come to the office the next morning at 10:00 a.m. Having spent so much time in the Maya municipality, I had become accustomed to not knowing what the purpose of my visit would be. Often, I would get a phone call in the morning to be at the office in five minutes. I would quickly pack a few things without any idea of what to expect or how long it would take and would often not return to my place until late at night or the next day after a long endeavor to the capital or other region.

From 2011 until the time of his passing in 2017, Don Tomás was the leader, "president," and highest ajq'ij of the Maya Quiché. He was voted into office by eighty-five community leaders from the district of Quiché. The official job description for the highest authority of the Maya people in Guatemala is Unabe Kamalbé of the Ancestral Maya National Council. Don Tomás was awarded this title for life in 2011 when his predecessor, José Macario, passed on. He also held the lifetime post of the Nim Winaq, the "first man" of his people, and was respected as the leader of all Maya in Guatemala by most of the other Maya tribes in the country, including the Garifuna in the Caribbean.

There were some individuals, however, looking for personal power and money from national and foreign governments as well as the UN, who did not approve of Don Tomás as the leader. No man is holy, and in Maya society, too, competition and envy are far-reaching problems that severely disrupt what could be Maya unity. These individuals often don't agree with the traditional requirements of being an ajq'ij, which puts them at odds with the traditional ancestral system and pushes them to create new ways around it.

I met with Josefa when she got out of work, and we ate at the market. You can have anything from a good beef stew to a simple tortilla, juicy and handmade in front of your eyes by women clapping the white, yellow, or black corn mass with their hands into a flat pancake, which then lands on the hot iron and is turned to bake nicely on both sides. Ideally, its inside stays soft while the outside is a little crispy.

⅞

Though we love to eat in Western society, we often do not give reverence to the food we consume. This is not so for the Maya, for whom food is filled with spirit and god given. They have a particularly deep respect for corn, as it is not merely a vegetable, but in the sense of "you are what you eat" their entire essence, making up their body and soul. Maize is the food of the gods, given to man by his ancestors to be consumed and honored. And mostly it is. The Maya respect their corn. They have been cultivating it for thousands of years. From sowing to harvesting, they work it precisely to the unwritten agricultural calendar, which includes instructions from the ancient "sky watchers," and observation of planetary transitions and natural phenomena, such as the flight of hawks (see Barbara Tedlock, 1992, for more information).

The ears of corn hang to dry at the owner's house and then sit for some time in storage rooms, where the owner sprinkles rum in the four corners or leaves a bottle of rum close by for protection and to honor the numinous powers. Then the kernels are loosened from the ears by hand, and the women mill and cook the corn for everyone in the household to consume. Some women keep to the ancient way of grinding it on the millstone, while others go to the corner store and have it ground in a small hand mill.

Many people, even in town, have a piece of land where they grow their own corn; one does not buy it at the market. It is a family tradition, an ancestral one, perhaps like the home production of olive oil or wine is to Italians. Italians who own olive trees or wineries are often suspicious of consumer products.

The Popol Vuh says that maize is what the Maya are made from. Few of the Maya have read the Popol Vuh, but through oral tradition, most know of it and live by its moral example. It states that the Creator and Framer of the world created life not once, but several times—first the animals, then man molded from clay and carved from wood—but every attempt was unsuccessful. The clay men melted in the sun or they neglected their reason for being—to worship their Creator—and needed to be destroyed and transformed (D. Tedlock 1996, 68; Smithsonian NMAI 2012).

Most recently, the deities made man from corn. We don't know whether the Creators were successful this time, because the era of man made from corn is ongoing, but since modern humans forget to worship their Creators, it can be assumed that man will be transformed again.

9/5

After Josefa and I had finished eating, we went up to a nearby restaurant called Don Pasqual. It was closed, but the owner, an acquaintance of Josefa's family, let us in. That day the Baile de las Chicas was to be danced. This dance is performed in all festivities throughout the Maya calendar year, and especially around every twenty-first of December, for fun and to honor the patron Santo Tomás. That night, the restaurant was reserved for the performing women so they could change into and out of their costumes away from the many eyes on the street.

While Josefa and I sipped a glass of Chilean red wine, the girls had their behind the scenes break time. The all-day performances left little time for meals and rest. There, sheltered from the crowds, the women were among their friends and family who helped them rid themselves of their masks and heavy costumes and slip back into their civil identity after having been submerged in a mythical one throughout the long performance. Many of the women were dressed as beautiful ancient Maya girls with masks resembling a mixture of Maya and European features and white skin color—a symbol of ideal beauty. (For a photo of the Baile de las Chicas, see plate 13.)

But these masks would not always have been white, nor would this have been a symbol of ideal beauty in ancient times. The syncretism melting different religious and historic cultures—the ancient Maya and the Christian—is ever-present in the various enactments. By obscuring historic truth and simultaneously making it transparent, it is confusing and enlightening alike. The function of these dances is to suspend time to enter mythic time so as to absorb and relive these encrypted messages. At the same time, the dances serve to lighten the horrific historic events and by doing so entertain the spectators. They are a religious, historic, and cultural mix of authentic primordial events and contemporary alterations and events.

Back in the restaurant, the performers' arms were adorned with gold-colored bracelets, their heads with feathers. When the masks depicting old faces were removed, young faces were revealed. In some cases, the costumes of young women had disguised big-breasted elder women in their daily wear. Exhausted but ecstatic, they fell into the soft restaurant seats, their features almost as vivid as those of the idealized masks.

Traditional dances are a vital part of Maya life. The Baile del Torito, Baile del Venado, Baile de los Mexicanos, and the Baile de los Conquistadores, to name a few, enact events that mix history and myth. But many of the Maya dances needed modernization to relate to contemporary society. In addition, new dances were created. One example is the Baile Popular, which features figures that merge Disney characters with local children's heroes, moving hand in hand through the designated streets. In Sololá, the district capital at Lake Atitlan, a favorite destination of American and European backpackers, this dance also incorporates the tourist intrusion—the figures' masks mimic white faces with crude-looking features and blond punk hair. Hanging from their behinds are hip-hop pants.

Back at the house later that evening as I wrote my notes of the day, I reflected on the vibrant colors, unfamiliar dance movements that pulled me into a mythical world, the fun I had with Josefa, and my strong bond with Don Tomás. The events of the day had effectively pulled me far back in time and centered me very much in the present. As I lay in my bed, I looked toward the future, wondering what the next day would bring and preparing myself by thinking about the administration's welcome ceremony for me.

7

THE WELCOME CEREMONY

December 19, 2014

I arrived at the office next to the main church promptly at 10:00 a.m. This room I call an office is really a sacred room of the Ancestral Maya National Council administration where the authorities meet, receive parishioners, and start their visits and processions. It is guarded all day by Don Manuel Choc, who is the master of ceremonies, and additional authorities on duty.

On important occasions a non-even number of Elders (usually three or five) stand behind the long altar table of the sacred room, with Don Tomás in the center. Their *varas* (rods of authority) lie before them in the midst of flower petals and sometimes rum on the altar below the framed picture of Christ that we kneel before every time we enter and leave the room.

As I walked in, Don Tomás was placing rose petals on the altar. He offered me a seat. Five Elders arrived, then Manuel Xiloj appeared, once again acting as my main translator to Don Tomás. He and Julio David, the administration's lawyer, have been a font of eloquent information about Maya life and culture from day one in New York.

As usual, I had no clear idea of what was to happen next, but never could I have imagined how important this day would be—the day of my official welcoming. My arrival had never before been taken so formally. I had been an official guest at the five-day-long New Era celebrations at Oxlajuj B'aqtun in 2012, but since our New York encounter, I had been treated as a friend and confidante. The only official welcomes I had seen had been given to national and foreign officials, while I stood to the side of the Maya administration, as (almost) one of them. (For a photo of the Maya administration giving me a welcome ceremony, see plate 14.)

Don Tomás greeted me officially, his words translated into Spanish by Manuel Xiloj. He said we would go to church to put up a candle for me. Before leaving, I handed over to Don Tomás, in the presence of the Elders, about ten photographs I had taken of the 2012 celebrations, developed in New York and framed simply, Maya style, while I was in Antigua the week before. To avoid provoking envy and competition, I never bring big gifts, because I worry that it might not go over well with those who believe that Don Tomás has some kind of a financial advantage in my presence. Also, I want to continue to be treated as the friend I am and not as an employee of an NGO or other foreign organization, there to provide funds to the administration. However, I did bring a gift for Marizita, "little Mariza," a small orange handbag with a decorative rose, which made Don Tomás melt. I am grateful that their culture and presence has turned my stone-cold New York heart back into the loving one it once was. I was to experience this transformation of heart again in my official welcome ceremony.

We knelt before the office altar so that Don Tomás could offer a small prayer, and then we left for the church. As the guest of honor, I was to go ahead with Don Tomás, but, humbled, I stayed back a bit, letting Don Tomás lead while the Elders and I followed. We ascended the steep stairs to the church.

On the stairs, Elder male and female shaman-priests and -priestesses swung jars with burning incense and spoke prayers to the ancestors who were believed to exist below. The pyramidial stairs symbolize a sacred mountain, where the ancestors reside. Both pyramid and mountain resemble the form that to the Maya is the shape of the upper numinous part of the cosmos.

✑

The Maya believe that the Creator and Framer, together with Tepeu—the Sovereign Plumed Serpent—and the primordial grandparents, Xpiyacoc and Xmukané, gave form to our world (and our cosmos) out of a universe that was formless and in constant flux. Without this form, humans would live in chaos. The Creators also provided language, education, knowledge, and manners within traditions.

The numinous part of our world is shaped like a pyramid; the world inhabited by human beings is a square. Accordingly, in front of the pyramidal stairs with the church at the top, a square plaza provides space for traditions, business, and all other human endeavors. The fire in the shaman-priests' jars and in a fire pit on the bottom center part of the stairs never stops burning. Like the fire of the Olympics, it represents the eternal flame, which ensures life.

By talking into a pyramid, mountain, or any other altar, the Maya create a dialogue similar to the oracle at Delphi: the Greeks spoke to it, and eventually it answered back. Such a place becomes a mountain of words and, more importantly, intentions. Once intentions are set there, they exist in reality, though without any reference in time. In Absolute Time, time as humans imagine it is an invention. At an altar or oracle, all that is said and done, past and present, happens at once. There is no chronology of time. All the people who ever spoke in this place—or any other—are now present here, beyond time. Certainly their intentions are. One could say that after they died they stayed around to talk back to the living, to respond to their inquiries. Westerners have gotten so used to seeing everything in linear time that we can hardly imagine things existing on their own, exempt from time and space. What we do should be more important than how much we do; content should be valued over quantity, but this is difficult in a world that makes time run ever faster. The content and act of repetition and insisting, for instance through prayer, may be a much more important historical quest than that of measuring time and space. In other words, filling space and time with life off the clock is more meaningful than living by the clock.

☙

Our group proceeded to the Santo Tomás church for my official welcome ceremony. With the Maya leader in front, we knelt before the incense-enhanced entrance at the top of the pyramidal stairs. Inside we knelt once again upon entering the main hall and before the long ancestral floor altars where Maya parishioners lit candles and prayed to their ancestors and saints. We walked toward the main front altar, where we knelt again before the three patron icons.

The Elders witnessed the ceremony from the choir seats on the left. Those seats are reserved for them or for representatives of the Christian church when they come to visit Chichicastenango.

Don Tomás had me kneel to the side of the three town patrons in front of the altar. He took three long white candles out of the sacred pouch that every shaman-priest carries over his shoulder at all times and prayed to Santo Tomás. Turning to me, he moved his hand over my head and spoke long soft prayers, holding the candles over my head and shoulders. He had me kiss them before setting them to the side of the low ancestors' altar, where he bent down to light them. All of those actions served to purify and protect me while I was in Quiché and beyond. It may sound strange, but only someone who has experienced it knows that it works. Don Tomás's blessings truly purified my heart. Every time he spoke his prayers over my head, it felt like I was being exorcised from industrial New York City's craziness.

Our group left the church in the same way we entered. Down the stairs and past the ajq'ijab swinging incense jars, we walked along the side of the church to the upper office. Along the way I found out that we were going to attend an official celebration. We arrived at the Maya municipality's property. Although the administration holds the deed to the property, they have to fight for ownership with Telgua, the Mexican Guatemalan phone company that claims the terrain to be theirs. The land had been sold to the company by some corrupt official during the war years when Maya ownership meant nothing, and Telgua had built the local cell phone tower on this elevated, central property that was sacred to the Maya. Each party insists that the space is theirs to use: Telgua for their cell tower; the Maya for their traditional festivities, such as the one we came to take part in that day.

We walked by the attending guests on the dusty patio and entered a tent, going straight to kneel before Santo Tomás. The icon had been carried out of the church at 11:00 a.m. and conveyed in a procession that moved around the center of town in a counterclockwise direction, which represented the natural direction in which energy rotates around a vortex in that part of the world. The icon had arrived here to be honored by this year's alcalde, the mayor of the Santo Tomás brotherhood, who had cared for it this past year and who would continue to do so until a new mayor was sworn in on December 21 and took over the duty for the following year.

We sat at a long table with Don Gonzales, the current Santo Tomás alcalde. Don Tomás talked to him extensively. Then men brought beers and Coca-Cola, and Don Tomás was happy to see that there was even rum. Manuel told me that it was the proper moment for me to join the two men so that Don Tomás could present me to the mayor, who had invited us to this festivity. I thanked the mayor for the invitation, and he blessed me and my family. I handed him fifty quetzales (about seven US dollars) for the lunch. With my contribution, I showed respect to the authorities. My act translated to the community, and most people felt that if Don Tomás trusted a foreigner then they could also trust that person.

My position was special, but Don Tomás generally kept good relations with everyone, including the white Guatemalans, who, with their mostly exploitive industries, are often responsible for the poverty and lack of sovereignty of the Maya majority of the country.

A soup of beef and hen was served. I sat with Don Manuel Choc, the organizer and master of ceremonies of every festivity in town. He knows all the traditions in detail, including which steps to take and which dress to wear. On my other side sat Manuel Xiloj; we talked, as always, about many things.

Then in came Maquito, a young man I have known since 2012. He works in his father's transportation business and is Don Tomás's chauffeur, taking him to the capital at 5:00 a.m. and bringing him back at midnight. I have been with them on several such trips, and Maquito and I once spent hours waiting for the administrative team due to an error in planning, and we didn't manage to meet up with them. We had meant to attend a congressional meeting in Guatemala City during which the team intended to push their cause of bringing home the Popol Vuh, which had been housed in the Newberry Library in Chicago for centuries. Don Tomás's Maya administration felt that bringing it back to Chichicastenango, where it was written in the sixteenth century, would help to reestablish Maya rights.

To reach this goal was one of the issues for which Don Tomás and his team had gone to Chicago back in 2011 to plead the cause. Don Tomás had prayed before the holy book, in the bunkered basement of the library. He had asked it to come home—not an unusual request when you consider things to be living beings or items through which ancestral will can be moved. Because of that visit, a special room, financed by the American embassy, was constructed in the church convent where it once was written. An assistant of the then American ambassador, however, confided to me that they did not believe the Newberry book to be the only copy. Instead, they thought that the original book was in some private collection of one of the rich people in Guatemala.

Whatever the truth was, the little room in the convent could hardly protect this book of immense world value. How many armed men would be necessary to protect it from smart thieves who knew they could get big dollars for it on the international antique market? The already stressed soul of the town would be changed forever, and not for the better. As of this writing, the book remains in Chicago.

The day Maquito and I had missed meeting up with the team, I invited Maquito to see the interior of the nearby National Palace. I had been there many times and even lived a few streets down from it during one of the years that I lived in Guatemala between 1995 and 2001, when the historic center was still in its warlike phase—dirty and dangerous, but also very real and poetic.

Maquito, like most of the Maya, had never been inside the National Palace. The guards weren't likely to even let them in to the part of the building that was publicly accessible. As we walked around, I explained to him the historic battles painted in the wall murals over the entrance staircase. There were also paintings by famous Guatemalan artists that, sadly, I as a European knew better than many people living there.

Remembering these shared experiences, I smiled to see Maquito in the tent that day in Chichi (Chichicastenango). And as it turned out, Don Gonzales was his father.

Soon after the day's honorable meal in the tent was finished, Don Tomás got up and said good-bye to Don Gonzales. We all knelt before the Santo Tomás church and walked back down to the altar office, where we took pictures of everyone present, including the new Maya beauty queen, much like we had done in 2012.

Afterward, I met up with Manuel Xiloj, and we went to one of the local hotels to have a Cuba Libre and reminisce about their previous visit to New York. We talked about politics and personal things. As I mentioned earlier, Manuel was Josefa's younger brother. He was an accomplished machine engineer, educated at a Belgian university. His father had built a successful transportation business in Chichicastenango, so he could afford to send his son to Europe to study. Manuel supported his three children by taking French tourists through Guatemala. Additionally, he held an honorable and demanding position as Don Tomás's scribe and general manager.

Being the excellent diplomat that he was, he managed all the relations with foreign governments in and outside the country. He was the managerial pole of stability on official trips to the capital and other districts and countries. He took care of political and other visitors to Chichicastenango, and he moderated the five-day event around Oxlajuj B'aqtun, which was attended by hundreds of people. His colleague Julio David Diaz Chay managed the legal affairs. None of Don Tomás's team got paid. They all relied on the distribution of some national funds and their ability to acquire funds from international organizations.

Manuel's communicative talent and language skills helped to keep the administration running. He was the bridge for foreign or national visitors to this sometimes seemingly scary and foreign Maya culture. Don Tomás would call Manuel at 5:00 a.m. to discuss the daily agenda, and before 8:00 a.m., Manuel would be at the leader's house to read to him from the newspapers, since Don Tomás did not read or write. As he said, "This is what I have my boys for. They paint the words I say."

Then, the daily endeavors would begin, and all of the team were engaged—for their people—until late into the night. Did they sometimes go to nice restaurants? Yes, but when working long hours and dealing with ministers and the president on a number of sensitive issues for their communities, one would expect that they, at least on those trips, would agree to live somewhat better. The common man often criticizes politicians for abusing their positions, but they forget that large issues sometimes ask one to live larger as well.

As for Manuel, it takes a certain personality to be the leader's right hand, but by the same token, such a personality brings envy and distrust. It didn't surprise me to learn in 2016 that after all he did for his people, for very little in return, Manuel lost the trust of some Elders and had lost his position. He died in November 2017 of cancer.

Unfortunately, after his dismissal, the administration was not able to function at its high level without his expertise. The team was broken, and I knew the people who were celebrating this disruption. Pettiness does not pay off.

When Manuel went back to work that afternoon, I met Josefa Xiloj's sister Manuela for the Baile Regional, to be performed that afternoon at the bottom of the hill, which was one of its many stations throughout town. From far away, I could hear the traditional music sounding from gigantic loudspeakers. The dancers were already in full swing in the middle of the street, which was blocked off from traffic. It was not hard to make out Manuela's beautiful face in the crowd. She had been a teacher in a local school for more than thirty years, but working with children for so long had not taken her beautiful fine skin or life energy away; quite the opposite, in fact.

Josefa joined us soon after from her nearby office. The three of us watched the movement of the multicolored group of figures, dressed in typical Maya dresses from different regions and masks of grotesque faces. (For a photo of the Baile Regional, see plate 15.) Their huipiles were woven from thick thread and embroidered with elaborate structural or floral patterns, depending on which Maya region they represented. The one from Chichicastenango has a star bordering the neckline, which highlights the woman's head as the crown of creation.

There is a whole industry in the town for fabricating the costumes and masks for these performances. The knowledge of how to create ritual clothing is handed down within the family. The *talleres,* or workshops, are filled with materials to be used traditionally and, occasionally, with a little modernization.

Several of the female characters were danced by men, which resulted in yet another bizarre corporeal form and set of movements, creating a mélange of the real and the theatrical. The clothes, together with the accentuated masks, moved vividly to the music in the afternoon sun.

When the dance ended and the crowd dissolved, Josefa and I walked up the hill and through the Arco Q'uq'umatz, the massive ten-meter-high town portal and symbol of the town. We crossed the market and walked by the main church, into the eastern part of town, and up another steep stone-plastered hill, where, out of breath, we finally knocked on a door.

A boy opened it and let us in to the dark inner entrance area. His mother, Marta, came in from the back wearing one of the most beautifully worked huipiles I had ever seen. She had made it herself, and we had come here so that she and Josefa could talk about having her make one for Josefa as well. It took about three months to weave and embroider a lovely piece like hers, which made it expensive and valuable.

Josefa introduced me, and the two women spoke about the look of the piece in question, and other things that I could only guess at, since they mostly spoke in Quiché. Josefa also told me that Marta was an ajq'ij, so I assumed that Marta answered Josefa's personal questions as well. A year later, I would find out that Marta was initiated by the same shaman-priestess who would teach and initiate me.

We descended back to the center to eat dinner at Juan's shop in the market.

8

VISITS, PAST AND PRESENT

December 20, 2014

Josefa's daughter Shilon and son Canek were visiting from the capital. After studying in Guatemala City, Shilon had gotten a job as a chemist with Cementos Progreso. In the morning, Shilon sent me to her hairdresser friend to have my hair done—a rare treat for me here in the highlands. The good girl did not know I was specially protected by the Maya authorities, and perhaps she couldn't have cared less if she did. Seeing me as a white visitor, she charged me almost a New York–like fortune. In the Maya lands, women wear their hair long and tend to it themselves or within the family, unlike in other countries, where one finds a hairdresser on every corner.

I met Josefa and her children in town, and we walked to the cemetery. I wanted to visit the grave of Doña Anastasia, Josefa's mother. Josefa wasn't fond of going, because she felt that her mother lived in the house with her—and she was right—but she wanted to do me the favor, so we went.

I wanted to pay my respects to a woman whom I had known briefly but with whom I shared a bond of friendship. Although we had eventually liked each other a lot, when Josefa had first told her that I, a white foreigner, would be staying with them, she had been suspicious.

On the day I first met Doña Anastasia, when I got to the house, she was sitting in a chair on the patio, loosening the harvested corn from its ear. We could not talk, since she only spoke Quiché, so I sat down in the doorway and began loosening corn with her. I noticed that the corn ears were piled up in a corner of the patio and beside them stood bottles of rum, which were meant for the corn spirit, as I learned later.

We sat like this for quite a while and little by little got closer. At night I cooked a chicken dish, and we drank from the half bottle of rum I had brought. That did the rest. We got a little loose and happy and, with Josefa translating, had a lot of fun.

Via her daughter, Mama Anastasia told me about her upbringing and how poor her family had been. She and her siblings used to sit beside the avocado tree waiting for one to fall down. Then they all ran for it. They had to win the race against each other, but mostly against the dog, who was usually the fastest and got to have the fruit all to himself.

Doña Anastasia died in May 2013. I could not come for her funeral, but her soul is in the house and in her room, which I would occupy for a month in 2015, when I returned to train to become a shaman-priestess.

9

MEETING MY MENTOR, DOÑA TOMASA

December 21–22, 2014

Finally, the day of the patron's celebration had come once again. Although I typically took part in all the Santo Tomás festivities, some of the year's events took place too far from Josefa's house for me to walk back at night, and there were no taxis between 9 p.m. and 9 a.m., so I did not participate in the night ceremonies as I usually did.

We all remembered the year 2012 and the beginning of the new cosmic cycle, that of Oxlajuj B'aqtun, the Thirteenth B'aqtun, a cycle of 5,125 years, which simultaneously began an even larger cycle of 26,000 years. We stand at the beginning of the fifth of five times 5,125 years, the cycle of ether (Barrios 2009). Having been an active member in the 2012 transition and celebration now, in 2014, I am again, as every year, invited to participate. Having been an active member in the 2012 transition, I am almost expected to participate every year and not break the cycle once initiated. And 2014 was no exception.

Throughout the day, the processions with the saint icons were in full swing. Today was also the day when the mayors of the three brotherhoods of the patrons Santo Tomás, San José, and San Sebastian would hand over their varas to their successors for the year to come.

The national mayor, who was hired by the Guatemalan state, hosted an official lunch in the town's theater. I attended, and next to me sat a couple who ended up inviting me to a shaman's house later that afternoon.

The shaman's name was Doña Tomasa, and to get to her home, about four miles away in the direction of Santa Cruz, we took a three-wheeled tuk-tuk. We drove for ten minutes before a conglomeration of three buildings and a cement two-story house appeared.

The driver left us off, and we were greeted by a crowd of Doña Tomasa's grandchildren of all ages and some of her daughters. A boarded door at one of the buildings squeaked open, and a small woman with long salt-and-pepper hair appeared. Her body seemed both solid and fragile. Her smile was friendly, but the authority of this well-known ajq'ij kept me on alert. (For a photo of Doña Tomasa, see plate 16.)

A smile spread across her face, and she welcomed us warmly, her heart open, her spirit shining toward us. She showed the way into the hut. As we entered behind her through the little door, a hall opened before us with a long table and wooden bench and a beautiful altar at its end. On it were flowers, lit candles, and several small images of Jesus Christ as well as a larger framed image of the Virgin of Guadalupe. Later I learned that people came to this altar from near and far and that the healing forces of both Doña Tomasa and her daughter Sebastiana, and the presence of the Virgin, are widely sought.

After she attended to my new friends, I was left alone in the room with Doña Tomasa. I started telling her a little about myself.

She looked at me and said, "You need to get initiated." I knew she was referring to the process of training to be an ajq'ij, or daykeeper.

Surprised, I said, "No, I don't think so."

"Yes, you do," she replied with the same warmness and rays of light that shined from her when she welcomed us.

I don't remember any more of our conversation, and I think that was more or less it. I hadn't gone there to hear this assertion. The most I had hoped for was to get a little visionary insight into some minor issues in my life, so this message of responsibility was very unexpected. There was realization in my mind that by taking this step my life would turn around. I grew up in various cultures and speak four languages daily with people across the world. Despite consciously feeling and knowing that the Maya world has always been a part of me, how much would I be able to absorb? How deeply would I be able to identify with the Maya, and how practically could I incorporate this identity into my life? After all, I did need to live in the Western world again. I needed to think about it, and so we agreed to meet in town the next day.

DECEMBER 22, 2014

To get to know each other, to receive more information, and ultimately to reach a decision about whether to become initiated as an ajq'ij, I was ready to meet again. I had anxiously but thoughtfully waited all morning for my reencounter with Doña Tomasa and her daughter Sebastiana, whom they lovingly call Poxita. I met them at the San Juan restaurant around noon, and we talked about our lives and discussed my future shamanistic training. Our meeting was joyful, like something long expected that opened a portal to the future.

During our conversation, I realized that they were well-known Maya shaman-priestesses who had been invited to the United States to participate in important international shamanistic meetings.

They were very sweet to me and welcomed me to the family. To me this was awkward, since we didn't know each other. My Western self was suspicious of why Doña Tomasa had offered to initiate me, so I tested them. Among other questions, I asked what I could bring them from the United States. Sebastiana requested little shells or stones, if it was my will to bring them to her, which I thought was very humble. She passed my little test of material entanglement with ease. (For a photo of Sebastiana, see plate 17.)

Then I asked them what I would need for the training. They mentioned a sut, which is a head scarf woven in the traditional Maya patterns symbolizing the four corners of the world and that honors and protects the head and acts as a sign to others that you have been initiated or have some kind of authority within the Maya community. Further I would also need a faja—a belt representing the snake, which one wears under one's clothes at all times and maintains one's energy and protects one from bad spirits—and a bag for my instruments, stones, or whatever else I needed for my private fire ceremonies.

José Luis Tigüilá had already explained to me the basics of how to read fire, whether it was a full ceremonial blaze or just the flame of a single candle—either way, the results would be the same. If the flame tended to the east, where the sun rises, the answer was positive. If it leaned toward the west, things wouldn't go well. If it leaned north, it signified Imox, the nawal that indicates craziness and negativity. South stood for Iq', the wind. If the flame moved in this direction, the issue in question would go cold but could be worked on for the better. These were the theoretical fundamentals; in my apprenticeship with Doña Tomasa, I would learn more.

While I was listening to what Doña Tomasa and Sebastiana had to say, my spirit dove into an alternate space in which my identity seemed to merge with hers. I had a moment of mirror vision in which I saw myself as her, one day in the future, with her long hair, Maya face, and wisdom. So I asked her again if I should really be pursuing this course. She laughed kindly, free and wise, and said, "Yes, this is your path."

I expressed my doubts by telling her that I didn't think I had the power to battle the negative forces within me, and she told me that I would obtain the force with the initiation. She also said, "That of the outside is that of the inside," meaning that if one is positive inside, one has nothing to worry about or battle. There is no difference between inside and outside oneself; there is no border between the two dimensions.

Doña Tomasa and Sebastiana asked me not to talk about my training, probably so I would not give my force away or attract envy and give way to people who would want to do me wrong before I was initiated.

Of course, I had already told Josefa, José Luis, and Manuel Xiloj about my upcoming training and initiation before Doña Tomasa had asked me not to. I also told Doña Tomasa that I didn't keep secrets from Don Tomás. She specified not to talk about details, and I never did. When I told Manuel that I was going to be initiated, he was shocked. He said that he had seen people who could not manage the power and became alcoholics or went crazy. He also wondered about the intention of the people who were to train me. (He did not know who was to train me. Just to show how entangled people and things can be, I later found out that his wife was one of Doña Tomasa's daughters!) But at that point, I didn't tell him who my teacher would be, and he suggested that I prove my teacher's worthiness to myself. He said that if they lived north of Chichicastenango's east-west line it could go poorly for me and that I should observe how the people whom they trained before me were doing in their life. Were they successful, or not?

I knew Marta, Josefa's friend, who seemed to be a beautiful, friendly lady with two lovely and intelligent children, and I knew some others who seemed equally fine, so I felt relieved.

I dream a lot at night and often have visions and daydreams, and the night before I had dreamed that Doña Tomasa would want to exorcise me, like I felt Don Tomás did when he was giving me a blessing. It seemed to me that he was taking the New York City energies out of me and clearing my body and mind. And in our conversation that day, Sebastiana told me that I should expect strong emotions to come out of me during the ceremonies.

To receive clarity about undergoing the planned training, the previous night before falling asleep I asked the universe silently if I should really do it. The minute I asked the question, a Maya man appeared above me. He was dressed in a 1970s Guatemalan-style suit and a hat. His face was like wood. He was Rilaj Mam, also called San Simon or, more popularly, Maximón.

This Maya saint had been my protector since early December 2012, when I first went to see him high up in Santiago Atitlan. For a while I stayed and sat on the ground before this wise grandfather icon, lit candles, and fell into prayers. I never expected to receive a response—aren't the Maya saints reserved for the Maya only?—but I did. A feeling of connection and love overcame me, and although it was not a message in words or visions, it was miraculous. Since then, I have gone to see him wherever he is housed each year in Santiago Atitlan.

In this new vision before I fell asleep, he sat on a simple low wooden chair like the Maya use in their houses, and he made a gesture with his hand as if to say, "Go ahead with the training. Do it." Rilaj Mam's gesture was crystal clear in this vision, and I had no more doubt after that affirmation. I had received ancestral permission. I thanked him. I did not know why I was supposed to get initiated, but I accepted this new path. Secretly, I was grateful; but at the same time, I recognized the great responsibility that would come with it.

This affirmation was one of many that I had received throughout the years, pointing me toward my future training as a Maya shaman-priestess. As a child I had dreamed that I was to decipher the Maya glyphs. Today I assume that it meant I was to decipher Maya spiritual meaning. And once as a teenager, an older Maya woman appeared to me in my room when I was sick. Since I grew up in Europe, I hardly knew anything about the Maya back then.

In 2001, before moving from Antigua, Guatemala, to live in New York for twelve years, I had another mythical dream. In it, I dreamed that I had to pass through twelve years at airports and hotels before returning "to the pyramids." I also dreamed of an arch with a strong light behind it. In the dream, I had to sweep in front of the door to my home and harvest the apples in my parent's garden before I could pass through the arch. For years I feared that the arch signified death. Never would I have thought that it signified the entry arch of Chichicastenango, a town that in 2001 was as foreign to me as any other far-flung place in the world, but one that would become important to me in the future.

Another affirmative dream occurred in 2013 at Don Juan Camajay's house. Tata Juan, the second most important man of the Maya spiritual-political hierarchy, had invited me to his village. It was strange, because on that day I should have been with Don Tomás at a TV filming of a typical festive meal that the administration would eat at festivities. But I decided not to participate in the filming and instead took the three-hour bus ride to Tata Juan's village. Twice the bus got stuck, and I should have known to turn back. I didn't. It took much longer than normal to get there, but I finally did. After meeting the town officials, visiting the church, and praying at the Maya altar, Tata Juan invited me to lunch at his house. After some general conversation, I asked if I had some task with the Maya. The answer came immediately, though not from Tata Juan. Instead it arrived as a thought from Above into my mind, and it was a simple, strong, clear "Yes."

There were many dreams pointing to the future, so I felt confident establishing the date on which to begin my initiation training with Doña Tomasa and Sebastiana. Near the end of our conversation at the San Juan restaurant that day, the three of us counted backward in the Maya calendar, since training should always conclude on the day of gratitude in its highest frequency. I would have liked to begin on February 18, 2015, but it coincided with Wajxaqib' B'atz', and in the week before this calendar day of new beginnings, all ajq'ijab go inward, and no ceremonies take place. So we picked a specific day in March,* and Sebastiana said that she wanted to graduate me personally and hand over to me the pouch containing the sacred Tz'ité, which is every ajq'ij's medium for divining messages from the ancestor and spiritual energies.

We talked some more about the initiation process, and Sebastiana summarized: "It will be your Maya incarnation."

I would be back in March to begin the training.

---

*There will be more about the qualities of the day energies in part 3 of this book.

10

SANTO TOMÁS CHANGES COFRADIA

December 22, 2014

In the mornings I often spent time with friends or the administration. When I returned to begin the initiation process, I would typically spend the morning hours with Doña Tomasa and Sebastina, then participate in the cultural life of the town in the afternoon. This particular day was another busy day for the administration. It had begun at 5:00 a.m. with the ceremony and election of the new authorities of the Maya administration, the Autoridades Ancestrales de la Alcaldia Indigena. The elected men would take their places on January 1.

The mayors of the other municipal communities had arrived with their assistants the night before and needed to be attended by the administration. Bands were playing and fireworks had been exploding since dawn. The town was bustling; it was loud, crowded, and busy.

Since 9:00 a.m. Don Tomás and his entourage were engaged in the change of the brotherhood of Santo Tomás. Every saint (icon) has a brotherhood (*cofradia*) to take care of him throughout the year and grant the community access for prayer. With marimba, drum, and chirimia music playing, through the incense-laden streets Don Tomás led the first mayor of the new Santo Tomás brotherhood, the honorable carriers of the icons, the local authorities of the eighty-seven communities, and the shaman-priests, dancers, musicians, invitees, and attending community in a circle around the market and town for an hour and a half until they arrived at a street down the hill to enter Santo Tomás's new home. This coming year, the patron's new brotherhood would be on this street near the cemetery, where his newly voted-in Mayor Domus lived. Santo Tomás would be placed here in a specially dedicated room, where devotees could visit him throughout the following year. Many of them would have personal encounters with the saint, as would I.

That afternoon, after my meeting with Doña Tomasa and Sebastiana, I went there to attend the handing over of the saint to a new brotherhood. The icons were staged in front of the property all by themselves on the street—a strange site, considering the amounts of people around them usually. Where was everybody? I peeked in by the gate and saw that the place was packed with about a hundred invitees.

From the bright sunlit patio, I entered into the sacred room where Santo Tomás would be placed later on and where he would stay for 365 days. Tomorrow there would be another celebration in which his new clothes, carefully fabricated by one of the town's ritual clothing specialists, would be presented. On benches around the walls of the dark room sat about fifty men of the brotherhood dressed in the black-and-red tradition of Chichicastenango. In their midst sat Don Tomás, whose hand I kissed respectfully. I also kissed the new Mayor Domo's hand respectfully and waved greetings to the other men.

The ritual dancer carrying Tzijolaj moved around the room. He danced up to me and tapped the pouch that was bound to the wooden rider's horse. I pulled out a bill from my wallet and placed it, as expected, in the little pouch of the icon. The dancer smiled, content, and gave me a wet kiss on the cheek. I tried to wipe it off unnoticed, but everyone noticed, and the *cofrades* (brothers and/or elders), burst out in laughter.

The ice was broken once again, even with those who didn't yet know me. People here have seen so much sorrow, and the calendar rituals are repetitive, so any reason for a good laugh is welcome. All the festivities that seem new and exciting to an outsider are a serious responsibility and a lot of work for the administration and the brotherhoods. The events of the yearly calendar must be executed in the utmost detail, and there were many of them throughout the year. Although the Maya value repetition, they also love anything that brings a little change to their ritualistic, authoritarian, male routine, and that little lady from a foreign country did just that.

Back on the patio, *atol de jicara*—the sacred hot corn beverage, also called *pox* (pronounced posh)—was served to everyone. The women had cooked it in large boilers and then brought it from the back of the house to the patio, where they poured it into small clay cups, which were passed from attendee to attendee until everyone had one.

When the cup came to me, I swallowed the first sip and almost fainted. To this day I still don't know if there were germs in it or if the beverage just had a strong spiritual effect on me. But I certainly felt immediately that I was part of the community and spirit. It was similar to but more intense than taking the *hostia* (body of Christ) in a Christian church.

The women, especially, got a kick out of seeing me, a white person, drinking the traditional beverage. I laughed and chatted with them, although many were unfamiliar with the Spanish language. We sat on the long bench, and the special occasion bonded all of us together, making us feel as one. It was quite amazing that they had taken me in, considering that these people all had family members or friends who had been killed by white people in the recent past during the guerrilla war. Not every Maya was a forgiving or otherwise holy person, but the notion of forgiveness and peace was something they all grew up with and fostered every day of their lives. I was grateful for their warmth and open acceptance of me personally and in my role as an "ambassador" of the Euro-American culture.

Though I only had that day left in Guatemala, I felt intrigued by what my next visit to the country would bring.

PART 3

THE SPIRITUAL
JOURNEY

11

WHAT IT MEANS TO BE INITIATED AS A DAYKEEPER

An initiation is a rite of passage in which one is reborn into a new identity, but for me, my initiation was not so much about being reborn as a Maya because somehow I had felt a little Maya from childhood on, long before my first encounter. The shaman-priestess identity, however, was deeply buried within myself and obstructed by the influence of Western culture.

Much has been written about initiations from various continents and cultures. In the following chapter, my aim is to widen the usual perception of a consecration based on my personal experiences.

Before the initiation process can begin, the numinous powers must grant the teacher and the student permission for consecration. The assimilation of the Maya spiritual heritage, however, is a process that happens before and long after the single day of formal consecration. During the entire process of performing daily fire ceremonies that leads up to the initiation, the novice becomes linked to the numinous powers—the energies of the Cholq'ij calendar days (nawales)—by repetitively counting the days connected to these powers until a spiritual connection with them occurs, and the novice feels them inside his or her body and starts feeling, hearing, or seeing messages.

Nawales can be compared to telluric energies, ancestors, unnamed planet energies, saints, or Christian sacred beings, all of which are forces of one God, Ahau. The nawales amount to 260 days signs; they represent the twenty energies times the thirteen frequencies or levels of strength or vibrations of the Cholq'ij calendar. The novice is not confronted all at once with these energies, but rather daily, one by one, throughout the 260-day initiation process. It is these forces who lend him their own animal (or other) abilities, superior to man, which involve flying, being able to see "around the corner" and at night, surviving a long time without eating, and having a strong intuition, to name but a few of the characteristics.

Encounters with the Sacred may or may not be terrifying, but the disciple needs to be prepared to ensure that he will not fall into a state of fear. Suffering fear when facing what could be an alarming unknown must not be part of the formal consecration act at all. For this reason, many initiators usually ask a main sacred being to confront the courageous novice during the initiation. Face to face, the novice becomes familiar with that force and recognizes it later on.

Basically, I recognize two different kinds of individual disposition, which can lead to two very distinct kinds of initiation. Depending on one's personal disposition and birth energy, one may tend more toward either ascending into the heavens and communicating with those forces or descending into the underworld and having a stronger relationship there.

In *Rites and Symbols of Initiation,* Mircea Eliade distinguishes the two kinds of initiations and describes the individual origin of the two spiritual experiences.

> The initiatory theme of ascent to heaven differs radically from that of the swallowing monster; but although, in all probability, they originally belonged to different types of culture, we today often find them together in the same religion; even more, the two themes sometimes meet during the initiation of a single individual. The reason for this is quite evident: the descent to the underworld and the

ascent to heaven obviously denote different religious experiences; but the two experiences spectacularly prove that he who has undergone them has transcended the secular condition of humanity and that his behavior is purely that of a spirit. (1994, 128)

The preference for either ascending or descending seems to be determined by an individual's nawal, or day sign, as much as by one's temperament. It would be a subject to study, if ajq'ijab born under signs such as the bird energy (Tz'ikin) are lighthearted and would rather fly upward, while those born under the jaguar (I'x) have a rather mystical character and prefer to descend. I assume that Maya administrations typically have members of ascending and descending natures in balance. Just as the globe must balance Sky and Earth, so too must these elements be balanced in Maya government. As the head of the Maya Quiché, Don Tomás represents the upper connection to the universe. The ascending ajq'ij may even correspond to the feathered serpent, Quetzalcoatl, and I wonder if it is a prerequisite for any *ajpop* (leader or, formerly, king) such as Don Tomás to be born under this sign. Because of my disposition and birth energy, I relate more to the ascending.

The initiation may happen in public or in private (Eliade 1994, 143). Anthropology mostly has testimony of public initiations. The private part may happen while the disciple is roaming the desert or the woods, or it may occur in dreams and visions when the disciple receives the calling, which is often the first part of the initiation. Sometimes the novice also gets instructions from the numinous force or his or her ancestors directly.

During the initiation, the disciple becomes linked to the sacred forces. At the same time or possibly before the link occurs, the novice also undergoes instruction in how to pray and receives knowledge of how to see, feel, understand, and handle the numinous world. Through instruction, observation, and mimicking his teacher, the novice learns how to conduct ceremonies. The teacher constantly reaffirms with the numinous beings that the novice is worth the trouble.

Upon graduation, the apprentice takes on a mission for life in which he commits to the daily practice of cherishing the forces of the universe. It is the daykeepers' task to keep these forces alive (conscious within the human environment) and to keep the world in harmony. It is also their duty to be of assistance to people in need. Becoming or being an ajq'ij is not an easy undertaking. The counting of the days alone shows the hardship of the task. This repetitive process happens every day, or at the very least on certain days, and it is a long process in itself. The ajq'ij must seek communication with the numinous powers, and only sometimes do they come without the ajq'ij's doing so.

INITIATION AS A FORM OF DEATH

Present anthropologic knowledge often portrays initiation as a crisis. It tells us that during the initiation ceremony the novice is supposed to die as a regular person and be reborn as a shaman-priest/ess.

There are initiations in which terror, crisis, and death do not need to be a part. First of all, human beings undergo many unseen and unrecognized crises during their lives. Secondly, I am not convinced that nowadays things have to be as dramatic as in ancient times. After all, the Maya do not sacrifice human blood any longer, and chickens are now sacrificed instead of humans. There is such a thing as civilized ritual procedure today. The forms of symbolic death in ritual differ tremendously across cultures and have been integrated into modern society.

An initiation may substitute the enactment of a brutal death with a smoother form of passage. If the divine beings have accepted less dramatic sacrifices than human blood, why should a shaman-priest not spare his novice the death imitation and instead lead him or her to the other side in a gentler way? Death, even a ceremonial one, can be only symbolic after all. In rites of passage, it is nothing but a way to express transformation. I find this important, because it is what distinguishes contemporary societies—whether they are traditional or Western—from ancient traditional societies. While a ritual is based on the experience, contemporary societies tend to live more rationally. They have voluntarily moved away from the bodily experience of spirit toward an experience of spirit that is not felt through the body in a drastic way and is, rather, symbolic.

Many people, when dying, sail over to the other side quite peacefully. So why should an initiation ritual portray death only in the sense of suffering? Personally, I do not believe that death in consecration must incorporate the imagined shock and suffering, although in my true initiation, way before the formal one, it did, albeit in a vision rather than physical reality, as I will explain.

There may be as many different frequencies of intensity as there are frequencies of temperament in different people and cultures. Suffering in itself has different levels of intensity, and to the shaman-priest or -priestess can be experienced as the abstinence of food, sexuality, and company, which is a sacrifice required to be able to reach the level of sensibility that makes one capable of, not so much finessing willpower, but of becoming receptive to communication with the numinous beings.

Either way, for some, the "death" or other form of crisis and the following rebirth may be a sudden incident during the initiation. Others may have experienced it long before the initiation process. Many ajq'ijab go through a lot of illnesses in their childhood, and others have a near-death experience as adults.

One ajq'ij confessed to me that he had wanted to commit suicide because his business was going badly. He tried to hang himself in his house, but the attempt was unsuccessful; his assistant discovered him and came to his rescue. That incident, together with his birth sign and constant dreaming, disposed him to becoming an ajq'ij. Today, his business is going very well, and he hosts many traditional dancers for the various holidays that without him would not be economically possible in his town.

I once spoke to a Canadian woman in Florida who had had several near-death experiences—in an accident, while giving birth, and during a severe illness. She had also been in the Fort Lauderdale airport shooting in early 2017, but fortunately, she was only injured. These experiences are a sure sign that she is definitely well-suited for becoming a shaman. However, she wasn't aware of the opportunity because she did not know that the calling presents itself in this manner.

One may call it bad fate, but the Maya, as other cultures do, see such incidents as typical indicators of being called for spiritual service. If the person doesn't answer the call, bad luck in life and business or even death may occur.

Because of the Conquest, much of the Maya belief system has been lost and is now left to be filled in through inspirational imagination. In fact, much more needs to be imagined than what is actually being portrayed in the processions, dances, and devotions, which are really metaphors for hidden facets of truth. For example, the syncretized world of Christian saints who double for and mimic celestial occurrences is a network of secrecy in itself.

By the same token, we put way too much emphasis on the initiation occurring at a specific moment. The notion of immediacy aims to exalt drama just as the enactment of death does. But the Latin term *initium* translates as "training" or "beginning," which suggests that we are looking much more at a process than a moment. Similarly, the Maya apply the Spanish term *encaminarse,* meaning "to start walking" or "to get on one's way," to initiation because they also perceive it to be a process rather than a single moment or event.

The change resulting from the initiatory training affects the whole life of the disciple, so it seems rather unlikely that only momentary initiation must occur. On the contrary, changes do not always underlie an instant act of rapture but instead happen in a gradual process that comes into sight only over time.

Perhaps that is why, in contemporary societies, we quite often cannot observe our passages as we are going through them. As a matter of fact, even traditional societies set up the spectacle of an initiation only to mark a border. Not every African boy who goes through the painful experience of having ants crawl all over his body becomes a man in that instant. And not every Maya man or woman becomes an adult on the day that they turn a "13 x 4 person," meaning fifty-two years old, the age the Maya traditionally consider someone an adult.* Mircea Eliade, when referring to Australian rites of passage, said that "religious instruction does not end with initiation, but continues and has several degrees" (1994, 30).

The disciple acquires Maya spiritual heritage during the entire process of daily fire ceremonies. And yet another aspect needs to be taken into account. From personal experience, I believe that we need to ask, and this is mere speculation, whether the gender of the leading shaman-priest or -priestess may play a role in how initiations are conducted. In Guatemala initiations are mostly led by men. It seems to me that women may have other methods than some male shaman-priests.

A ritual of separation may be conducted in a softer and more subtle manner by a woman than it would be by a man. Ethnologist Leo Frobenius (1873–1938) displayed an interesting train of thought when he argued that male secret societies, societies of masks, were created during the matriarchal cycle to scare women. And Mircea Eliade suggested that by pretending to be demons, the men strived to "undermine the economic, social and religious supremacy" (1994, 121). Today anthropology acknowledges matrilineage but questions whether matriarchy ever existed, as Professor Bargatzky and other scholars explained in a recent interview on German radio B2.

Yes, women experience pain during menstruation and when they give birth, but they may see the initiation process more as a psychological one rather than one determined by the drastic, hands-on, public act performed for everyone to witness. Female ajq'ijab may allow the novice more freedom to experience initiation as a process, giving the disciple the time and space to develop like an embryo grows in the womb, unobserved by the community.

---

*Thirteen refers to the thirteen frequencies. Four refers to four cycles as well as the four corners of the world.

Perhaps, and only perhaps, social reality holds that life to many men is more of a fight, whereas to many women it can be the celebration of possibilities. After all, renewal to a woman is something of a monthly experience, or it can come in the form of a new pair of shoes, while to a man renewal is more rare and traditionally dramatic. As far as studies on women shamans go, there are very few indeed, if any; the existing evidence mostly involves male ajq'ijab. So it's difficult to compare the different approaches and come to a definite conclusion with any degree of confidence. I do, nevertheless, maintain the idea that the two different dispositions described above greatly affect how initiation is carried out and also regarded.

Initiation first and foremost means permission. For the Maya shamans, nothing happens without permission. The doorway is opened by the numinous powers. It is not the shaman-priest who initiates the novice but rather the nawales and ancestors. Once permission is given, and there is enough heart within the novice, things can begin to happen.

"Lifting one's heart" and "thankfulness" to a high frequency are the two most valuable concepts in Maya teaching. They link people back to the mythical substance they share, reminding them that all came from the Creator. Love may be the ultimate common substance. Without heart, humanity can still function—but like a machine.

Lifting one's heart can be achieved through prayer and spiritual practice, including spiritual fasting. By lifting one's heart, one raises their frequency to where Spirit is so as to harmonize with the spiritual world and hence make communication possible. To the Maya, people are in this world to show thankfulness to the forces that created us. We did not give life to ourselves, and we have only been given physical life by our parents.

The Maya perceive life as a give and take—an exchange. They see it as a contract between God and humans: God gives us life, and we cherish him and his many manifestations. Lifting one's heart enables one to communicate with the celestial forces. It is not a choice but a duty to keep this communication alive. Let us take care that our hearts do not harden.

The ajq'ijab who are in service to this connection between worlds made a vow to dedicate themselves to fill this relationship with life. Practicing thankfulness cultivates the heart and makes it soft, humble, and sensitive and, therefore, more loving. And cultivating the heart means cultivating oneself. Nobility comes with self-cultivation.

Looking at it from a Western perspective, the idea of cultivating oneself through art, music, and theater is certainly noble. But by Maya standards, without the spiritual depth and link to the Creator in a dialogue of reciprocity, it would be considered art for the sake of art, not the cultivation of Spirit.

Jewish people who seriously hold Shabbat know this. So do the Muslim believers, and of course Christians and all other believers in Asia and Africa who are serious about practicing spirituality.

Shabbat requires one to disengage from anything practical, especially when it comes to the use of one's hands. For one day of the week, such disengagement keeps one free to be receptive to Spirit. There is nothing wrong with working, but, as many religions teach, absolute rest in meditation is essential at times to remind ourselves that there are things that rule the world besides computers, cars, TVs, theaters, or books, which distract us from interacting with God and our fellow humans. The Maya don't practice a specific weekly day of rest. Nowadays, however, many Maya keep the Christian tradition of reserving Sunday for attending church and gathering with family.

While industrialized society, with its forced action and efficiency that often drive man toward a machinelike existence, frowns upon inactivity, the Maya consider sitting and "doing nothing" a tribute of respect to the numinous world. The body needs disengaged time to be filled with energy from the source. Not eating and not doing are ways to lighten the spirit and separate it from the body, letting it ascend and enhance spiritual communication with one's source. Many of the Maya carry out their work in the consciousness of the spiritual higher-ups.

It is undeniable that the Western business and employment model lacks the link to indispensable spirituality. Let us not forget that rationalism came into being in a century that followed extreme religiosity. It was embedded into a spiritual environment that no longer exists. Therefore rationalism today is a very different thing from that which the Enlightenment brought to the Western world. For the Maya, on the other hand, spirituality is not separate. It is tied into the work process like a thread is tied into a completed piece of woven material.

Technology seduces and distracts us from active life, and many are addicted to the escape it provides. Sadly, much in our society and media encourages such abuse rather than reporting about and cultivating activities that tie people to their community and to Earth and the heavens.

For many people in Western societies the idea of "practicing," as in "practicing yoga," consists purely of the physical aspects of the exercise—for instance, perfecting yoga poses. For the Maya "practice" is not practice unless it also includes staying in communication with one's source on a deep spiritual level.

Because they view the world this way, many Maya ask the numinous powers for permission for everything. Nothing is done without first calling upon the ancestors and asking for permission and blessings. Their link is real and existent. The Maya are aware that people on Earth have a limited view of things and need assistance. If an ajq'ijab tries to heal a person without permission from the ancestors or nawales, the patient might die. If a person consults the visionary Tz'ité seeds without having been initiated, he or she may become ill.

Don Tomás consults the ancestors for every major decision, be it related to government, the undertaking of a journey, or a healing. Permission ceremonies take place on the day that corresponds to the appropriate nawal energy of the problem presented. Don Tomás never acts on impulse; he waits for that day to come around, even if it has just passed within the twenty-day calendar, and it will take nineteen days for it to come around again. Only if and when permission is given, does he proceed. The shaman-priests from North America to South America work with this caution, as do the African, Australian, Middle and Far Eastern, and Siberian masters. Time is a factor to be respected.

Permission for an initiation means that the door is open. Still, you don't just make your way in; you ask for permission every step of the way. One must lift one's heart and make offerings for as long as it takes to get permission. Only when you have it, do you proceed.

You burn offerings to connect with the spirits.

You pray to remove all negative energies.

You lift your heart to reach a state of purity.

After all, every Maya ajq'ij will tell you that what really matters is not so much the initiation itself, but that you perform your obligatory ceremonies afterward. Performing a minimum of one ceremony every twenty days plus one on each of the days Toj, B'atz', and Ajmaq, as well as the day of one's own nawal (birthday) is considered essential so that the deal between the ajq'ij and the numinous powers is not interrupted. With each ceremony, the relationship grows, and the mission becomes stronger. As this happens, one effectively feels a calming effect, and the calmer one is, the stronger the relationship and mission become.

An indispensable duty of the ajq'ij is to maintain and strengthen the communication with the fire—to accurately read what the fire tells you and to go where it leads you. A newly initiated ajq'ij does not know how to read the fire on the day of graduation but learns it in the many months and years to come.

12

ARRIVAL AND ACCLIMATION

March 6, 2015 (3 Kan); March 7, 2015 (4 Kame);
March 8, 2015 (5 Kej)

Once again, I took the three-and-a-half-hour ride in the chicken bus from Guatemala City to Chichicastenango. It was peak rush hour with Friday-after-work traffic, and the streets were packed with buses and cars, all expelling clouds of black Third World exhaust.

The bus filled up quickly. I sat next to a young man who told me about his life as a construction worker, gardener, and security guard. Once a month, he took the bus from the capital of five million inhabitants to his hometown, Huehuetenango, a city that is situated even higher up in the mountains than where I was heading.

I also interacted with a mom and her baby sitting behind me, and I talked to a humble man from the Quichéan district capital, El Quiché, which, since the Spanish Conquest, also goes by the name of Santa Cruz. The town is a half-hour ride from Chichicastenango.

El Quiché, or rather Q'umarkaj, the archaeological site some five miles outside of today's town, is the former Maya capital. We know from historical literature that among the Maya, just as among any people, there were many quarrels and rebellions against the kings by their sons or other members of the government even before the European Conquest brought the culture to its knees. With the conquest of Q'umarkaj, many had to flee, and the nobility established the town of Chuwilá—"the town within craters"—also called Santo Tomás or Chichicastenango.

As explained earlier, Maya law and land are not congruent with national Guatemalan law and land, and so Santa Cruz today is the capital of the national Guatemalan administration in the district of El Quiché, and Chichicastenango is the Maya administrative capital where Don Tomás resided.

I arrived at my destination and got to Josefa's house at 7:00 p.m. to take her out to dinner. We went to one of the few restaurants in town, where we had grilled steak and rice with a sauce made from avocado and chicken stock.

Josefa was happy to have me staying with her. This time I didn't sleep in the living room. She gave me the room where her mother used to sleep when she was staying at the house. Josefa—and her children when they visited—had to pass through that room to the shower and bathroom, but other than that, it would be "my" room for the eight weeks of my stay. It would also be the only place I had privacy (or semi-privacy), where I would be away from the eyes of the people and be able to reflect on the ceremonies of my initiation process and receive dreams and visions and writings on the wall. Josefa had prepared the room with her sense of beauty and female tenderness, putting little flowers in a vase on the dresser to welcome me.

It was night, and I laid on the bed, relaxing from the long journey, the conversations, and the car exhaust. I felt a little worried about what was to come. Living in a world of constant cell phone reminders, I wondered whether Nana Tomasa had forgotten about me and the initiation.

She hadn't.

MARCH 7, 2015 (4 KAME)

I walked up to the town center to have breakfast on the balcony of the Don Pasqual restaurant, a wonderful place for people, scenery, food, and traditional decoration. It is set overlooking the town center with its lively market. During my long stays in the Maya mountains, restaurants served as a shelter and a bridge to my culture. But generally, I was granting myself a luxury that morning, since I wouldn't be dining in too many restaurants for the next eight weeks. I was there to interact with people, most of whom couldn't afford restaurants, so this wouldn't be where I would be spending my free time.

I took in the air flowing through the open windows as I admired the restaurant's traditional Guatemalan style and local textiles on the tables. I breathed in the atmosphere with its oil paintings by Guatemalan painters depicting Guatemalan landscapes. I enjoyed the simple but impeccable service and talked with the waiters and the owner, whom I had come to know during my frequent visits to the town.

My first task of the day was to visit the Santo Tomás church. I ascended the church steps, where the fire never stopped burning and where shaman-priests burned incense and spoke prayers. Inside, I introduced my presence to the spirits and paid my respects to Christian and Maya forces alike. White tourists who sometimes came here on their Christmas or Easter visit to Chichicastenango usually didn't kneel before the ancestors' altars, let alone light candles; I did. I used this practice to connect with the forces living around and protecting the town and its population.

Moving on to more worldly tasks, I left the church and entered the tarp-sheltered market stalls to buy vegetables and then looked for a butcher on the main road to buy some chicken for dinner. I also had a copy of the house key made.

Then I called Nana Tomasa. She said that she was in town and close by, running errands with her daughter Maribel, so I invited them to lunch. Maribel has Down syndrome but is a full member of the household, taking care of the children of her siblings and helping to do the dishes and laundry and everything else the women do to keep the place running. We had a nice lunch. I would begin my training with Nana Tomasa the next day, and she had it down in her calendar that she would officially present me to the nawales on the day 7 Toj, the day of fire, which would be Tuesday.

MARCH 8, 2015 (5 KEJ)

For breakfast, Josefa prepared sweet bread and eggs and cut papaya and cantaloupe. To drink, she cooked a sweet liquid corn mash. There may be coffee plantations in Guatemala, but the Maya whom I know rarely drink coffee, if at all. They drink their ancestral beverage, hot cacao. They consider coffee a beverage of the white people. They also consider sandwich bread and dinner rolls to be a food of white people, while the Maya eat corn tortillas.

Josefa told me where to pick up the minibus for my journey to Nana Tomasa's home. Many buses passed as I stood at the curbside and chatted with other people who were waiting to go to their office or job. The air was still cool at that time of the day. Buses came through the town arch and raced down the cobblestone hill, the driver's assistants hanging out the open bus doors and calling out the various destinations.

Finally, I took a bus that seemed to be going in the right direction. I had to bend more than the shorter Maya people to fit under the bus roof. I slowly squeezed into the one vacant seat in the very back row, which was packed with women returning from the market, carrying the bags and flowers that they had bought.

The bus stopped several times, and after about ten minutes the driver slammed on the brakes in the middle of nowhere, stating that this is where Nana Tomasa lived. Relieved, I made my way out of the overcrowded minibus and hopped out onto a dusty entryway that led through a low piece of wood resembling a fence.

Calling Nana Tomasa's name, I waited, and soon a young woman appeared and opened the gate. She led me between the two cement and stone structures at the front of the property: one housed storage for ceremonial material and the store she once ran out of the house, the other the toilet. For hygiene purposes, the Maya traditionally construct their toilets outside of the main house. There were also two outdoor washing sinks (*pilas*), where a young woman was hand-washing clothes.

As I walked along, another such building to the east of the dusty patio allowed me a peek into its very dark interior. This was the kitchen, and on another occasion, I would get to go in and see that it housed several stoves. The one room had no windows, only a small round opening in the tin roof for the sun to send its blessing beam onto the stove at exactly midday.

Behind the building was a three-story house that actually had a facade. This building contained the bedrooms. Next to it, in the back middle of the patio, under a tin roof, I saw the fire pit.

We entered the altar house to the west of the patio, and Nana Tomasa came to me and embraced me. We stood in the long, angular, windowless room where we had stood once before on my first visit, the long wooden bench and table to the left, and another on which baskets and bags could be seen to the right. The altar was placed at the very front of the room. It was a simple long table with all kinds of colorful items on it. As before, the large framed image of the Virgin of Guadeloupe stood at its center, waiting for people from faraway places to come and pray before her. Nana Tomasa was the Virgin's guardian.

Also on the altar stood a small cross. The symbol that has come to be connected exclusively with Christianity originated way before this world religion existed. In Maya belief, it symbolized the crossing of the north-south and east-west telluric energies—between the sun and the center of the Earth in its longitude, and the sunrise and sunset in its latitude. I would like to add my understanding of Jesus, the man on the cross. Leaving religion aside and looking at the Maya cross of telluric energies, I see the figure on the cross representing each individual in his or her life being on this crossroad of telluric energies at all times and places. No matter where we are, the cosmic energies are available to us. We are at this crossing at all times, and this is perhaps what the existence of Jesus means—he and we are God made flesh, and we live out God's energy in various ways within our lifetime.

Also on the altar were candles, a glass containing feathers, and vases of flowers placed to the north. The Maya use directions rather than the concepts of left and right when describing location, since every city, house, and item is located according to a corresponding direction that provides it with its energy.

Leaning in the corner were Nana Tomasa's and her students' sacred varas looking like colorfully painted walking sticks. And sitting on the altar were the students' five small woven bags filled with Tz'ité seeds, which remained on the altar throughout their training to absorb the sacred energy available there.

Below the altar sat candles and rocks that held the energy of certain nawales, and above it and to the right hung bunches of multicolored candles to be used in ceremonies. Adorning the cement-stone walls of the room were smaller framed images of Jesus Christ and the Christian pilgrimage church in the town of Esquipulas, in eastern Guatemala, along with pictures of the family and some friends.

Nana Tomasa was dressed in the typical thickly woven and embroidered Maya skirt and blouse (huipil). Her long hair was braided, and she wore an attractive amethyst necklace, probably a gift from a visitor or patient.

We sat down, and while peeling papaya and watermelon, we began to talk. Her cell phone interrupted our conversation. Ali, a former patient, was calling from Germany. Since I spoke German, I translated. He said that he was having an operation that day and asked Nana Tomasa to pray for him. When the conversation was over, Nana Tomasa led me to the altar. We knelt in front of the Virgin image and lit candles for Ali. In the form of prayers, she presented me to Ahau.

The door opened, and Nana Tomasa's daughters and five grandchildren entered. Her husband passed by outside on the patio. He is said to be more than a hundred years old. His passport says ninety, but they tell me that it was issued long after his birth, when nobody knew his real age. To me he looks about eighty-three.

The kids took me around the property and introduced me to the geese, turkey, and rabbits as well as Doggie, the fair-eyed dog that, when visitors come, stays in a cage. I played with the children while Nana Tomasa washed her hair in the outdoor sink. With her unbraided hair and jewelry, she looked like a young woman.

The rare, relaxing moment was soon over when some neighbors arrived, and we all sat down to lunch at the long table in the same altar room. From the kitchen building across the patio a daughter and a daughter-in-law brought a large pot with beef soup and filled everyone's clay bowl. Then they placed corn tamales and avocado halves onto our plates to accompany the soup.

After lunch, people started arriving to ask Nana Tomasa's advice. The ajq'ij vanished with them into another room. After a long while, the visitors left, and she and I sat and talked about my initiation process. She determined the hour of presentation with the day nawal, 7 Toj, which is when my first official ceremony would take place. During my past visit to Chichicastenango, we had planned my arrival time so that I would be in Guatemala for that particular day.

Nana Tomasa took me to the front room that faced the street. It had a glassless window secured with bars, which indicated that this part of the house functioned as a store, or had at some point. Wall to wall and floor to ceiling, the room was filled with all kinds of ceremonial materials. She showed me what we would be using for my daily ceremonies.

She seemed uncertain whether to ask me for money for the materials I would be using for my training, even though other ajq'ij did. From the perspective of the ancestors, the ajq'ij are not supposed to ask for money. Payment is supposed to come from the client's heart, and in my case it did. Nana Tomasa had a big family to feed, so I would certainly be giving her money daily.

When everything was set, I took the minibus back to town and Josefa's house and, as I did every day, wrote down the day's experience into my field research notebook. Later, I prepared a fish soup with shrimp, which sellers brought to the market from the coast twice a week, early in the morning. The meal was supposed to be for Josefa and me, so when her sister paid us a surprise visit and brought her daughter along, I was amazed—and relieved—that there was enough food to satisfy all of us.

13

WOMEN'S WISDOM
AT THE HEARTH

March 9, 2015 (6 Q'nil)

At 10:00 a.m. I walked to the town center to meet Josefa at her parents' former house. After her mother passed on, some of her sisters had kept rooms there so that they could have a place in the center of town. The house had several rooms with doors that opened onto the streets, so the sisters used the rooms as stores to sell textiles and local artists' paintings.

From there, Josefa and I took a minibus to her family's property in the village of Camanchaj, about fifteen minutes from Chichicastenango. This was where Josefa and her siblings were born, before the family moved to the town center.

The bus stopped by the village school, and we walked among the fields and up a dusty hill to their house. Josefa's parents had divided the property among their children, and next to the parental house, Josefa's other brothers and sisters had constructed their own houses on their part of the property. Donã Juana lived in the parents' house and watched over the property. She kept chickens and turkeys and managed the family's corn and beans that had been harvested the year before. She lived there alone, refusing to live with her children in the capital. The place seemed lonely, but all the family members visited her regularly.

When we arrived, Juana was preparing the thread that she would later weave into a Maya head scarf, or sut. Suts are worn by Maya authorities, and since this one was for a Maya therapist, Juana would use blue thread, blue like the cosmos. She also did custom weaving for a couple of Spaniards who sold her products abroad.

Josefa showed me into her parents' former main room where we stayed awhile in silence. We lit a candle, put some flowers in a vase, and honored the ancestors with prayers. This is always the first and last thing to do wherever one goes in the Maya world. Honoring the holy spirits and the ancestors keeps the communication channels alive and flowing and makes for a more connected life with those who have an overview of the bigger picture. I felt a lot of clarity, and when I called on Josefa's mother, the blood vibrated in my veins, which I took as a sign that my greeting and wishes were well received.

Juana prepared a hearty chicken soup for us in the large, simple, clean cement-brick kitchen that had a window overlooking the fields, which reached beyond the main road that we had come in on. Inside the kitchen Juana had a few simple pieces of wooden furniture and a wood-burning stove.

Maya women and men collect wood in the forest to be burned in the hearth for cooking and for warmth during the cooler months. For the Maya it is essential to one's well-being to be around fire as fire keeps humans connected to the natural mythical substance whose communication it facilitates. Women especially, pregnant or not, should keep their belly close to the fire to remain healthy. These are the things a physician will not tell you.

The stove is the central place for the family to gather. It is the primary source of light and life. Unlike an electrical energy source, the flames of real fire flicker, transmitting life and allowing spiritual forces to connect to the living people. Josefa's wood-burning stove replaced the once traditional hearth that Josefa's mother had when Josefa was a child in the house. Her mother, however, had approved of this stove, whereas she had never approved of the stove in Josefa's house in Chichicastenango, which, being run by gas rather than fire, interrupts the connectedness to the natural mythical substance.

The Maya see themselves as individuals who are interconnected in their community. While many Westerners try to escape this kind of connection, even young contemporary Maya mostly identify themselves as members of the system they belong to and with whom they share an identity, language, customs, and traditional apparel, along with a mythical substance representing the Maya people. The hearth symbolizes the origin of each family and all Maya people and their history. In Western society, man has stripped himself of the hearth, cooking, and ultimately the essence of fire. People in the West have opted for electricity instead, and I believe that much of their depression comes from the use of such unvarying, "dead" energy.

Feeling the presence of that lively fire in the stove, Juana's hands began to form tortillas from the corn mass. She threw the flat cakes onto the large metal plate of the wood-burning stove and turned them over just in time to keep them soft in the middle. I offered to help, but since it was my first time making tortillas, they didn't come out quite as round as Juana's. While I was working, I had to note that a white woman making tortillas was a rather unusual sight for these people. The parameters of class had been set since the Conquest, which meant that it was Maya women who worked as service personnel to the white people. No white woman would make tortillas, and hardly any would clean their house or do the laundry in the river or the pila.

On this day, though, we could break those rules to build bridges, and we bonded easily over the task, as is typical when women share housework. It is so grounding, and I am glad that my own mother taught me to engage in it. In this intercultural encounter, we were overcoming centuries-old boundaries. Around the stove, we understood each other, although Juana spoke exclusively Quiché, a language I had learned only a little.

Josefa's twenty-something-year-old son, Canek, arrived at the house, and we all sat down to lunch together. (For a photo of us eating lunch, see plate 18.)

After the meal, we gathered on the patio. The dog had been tied to a rope while we were visiting, and the chickens and turkeys ran around. Sacks of recently harvested corn lay under the roof of one of the buildings surrounding the patio. A mouse tried to eat the maize, and Juana grabbed a broom and went after him. There were lots of mice; they sensed that there was corn and had come to eat it.

Canek began to weigh the sacks of corn and black beans, which had been harvested on Josefa's part of the property. Most of it went to be sold at the market, fetching 400 quetzales per pound. The rest was for personal consumption throughout the year. I knew that it was not by chance that we gathered here today—the day the Maya calendar counted the day of the seed (Q'nil)—to inspect the beans and corn.

The 360-degree-view over the valleys was lovely. It was March, and the cherry trees were in full bloom. Juana brought out the dishes from lunch and washed them in the pila, which was usually filled by hand with water in the morning to be used throughout the day or week. A special soap from the supermarket served as dishwashing liquid and washing detergent alike.

The Maya do everything by hand, not because they cannot afford machines but because the use of machines just isn't customary and certainly not a way the ancestors would approve of, since it is a step removed from being connected to the Earth. In fact, many Maya women who have access to a river or lake still do their laundry in nature's water. Keeping to traditional methods is also a way to stay autonomous and removed from shortsighted and unapproved modern conveniences.

In the late afternoon, we returned to the house in Chichicastenango. Josefa's older sister, Manuela, dropped in to visit. We talked about the new Catholic priest who had just started working in town. Like all his predecessors, he wanted to rid the church of all the *costumbres,* the Maya customs and beliefs. He was set on eliminating the processions and brotherhoods, not wanting them to enter the church with any images, be they of Jesus Christ, Mother Mary, or any of the various saints. This issue would present another difficulty for Don Tomás and his team.

14

‖‖‖‖‖‖ ‖‖‖‖‖‖

MY INTRODUCTION
TO THE MAYA
CALENDAR ENERGIES

March 10, 2015 (7 Toj)

It was the day 7 Toj. In the Maya Cholq'ij calendar Toj is the energy of the element of fire, also called Ahau 7 Toj, (God 7 Fire). Since fire is so essential to life and its creation, Toj is a very important day sign. Due to its nature, it is also a dangerous one and therefore needs to be respected. Fire was given to people as a gift. It once was considered a miracle, so in the Maya world, Toj has become the day to show gratitude and is a day of offerings, including sacrifices. I learned from Nana Tomasa that on the path to becoming a daykeeper/shaman-priest, Toj is the day that disciples are traditionally presented to the nawales to initiate their consecration process. The nawales then accept the apprentice or not.

I arrived at Nana Tomasa's house to undergo this presentation. I found her in the altar room. Upon entering, I knelt before the image of the Virgin of Guadeloupe and spent a moment in gratitude. Then I met Nana Tomasa's daughter Pilar. To start a conversation, I asked what they thought about the new Christian priest in town. They said that there was no new priest.

I didn't understand. Later that day, I would go to see Julian, one of Don Tomás's administrators, who would tell me otherwise. Obviously, there is incongruence. At the administration I came to know that every new priest tries to eliminate the Maya syncretistic traditions. In further conversations with Nana Tomasa, I learned that she and part of her family did not agree with the costumbres of Don Tomás's municipality. I understood that many ajq'ijab didn't. They considered the syncretistic processions and the customs to be similar to theatrical performances that had nothing to do with Maya beliefs at all. Nana Tomasa also claimed that the nawales in the town museum, which was maintained by the Maya administration, were "badly treated." Instead of being on the ground in their corresponding directions and honored with flowers and specific attributes around them, these energy-holding rocks were in glass cases and were not being attended to. They had become museum objects. Among those neglected pieces, said Nana Tomasa, was a "beautiful nawal Imox," the eleventh-day energy of the calendar that had an energy that corresponded to creativity and water, neither of which were present in the museum setting. I agree with her that a more fitting museum concept should be considered.

Nana Tomasa and her daughter Sebastiana were supposed to conduct my initiation process. Nana Tomasa's other daughter Pilar was also present that day. We moved over to the patio and under the tin roof that covered an open space with a two-yard-wide fire pit in its center. Several rocks inhabited by certain nawales were placed around it permanently.

We brought mats, or *pops,* made from reeds and rushes to kneel on. When eating at a table, people sat on chairs. However, when conducting ceremonies, weaving, and doing other such tasks, these mats were used because they were essential for staying grounded, allowing one to keep the spine straight as an axis between Sky and Earth.

The mats have had a mythical significance in Maya life ever since the ancestors starting kneeling on their pops at ceremonies and official gatherings. Since then the mats serve to accumulate wisdom. It is on these mats, after all, where one communicates with the numinous powers and receives messages. Also, the Quiché Maya Book of Council holds all of the Maya wisdom. It is therefore called the Pop Vuh, or Popol Vuh, for like the mats, it represents the "seat of wisdom."

It was early morning, and we all came together in the sacred space around the fire. The space symbolizes the original, primordial, sacred world as the Creator intended it. When activated, it becomes a place apart from time and totally connected to the primordial substance. We stepped into this space clean and in our best state. Nana Tomasa, Sebastiana, and Pilar put their head scarfs on for protection from the wind energy that can bring illness to ajq'ij and as a sign to society and the numinous powers alike that they were shaman-priestesses. I wondered at how the Maya attire had progressed under Christian dominion from near nakedness to this thick cloth.

This scarf is reserved solely for its owner's head. It should not be worn by any other person, and it should not be used for anything other than to cover the head. Before the ceremonial fire, the ajq'ijab always wear ritual clothing and jewelry. Around the waist, they wear a red woven belt, which protects them from attacks by strong forces that like to hurt the kidneys. I have experienced the impact of these forces in several of the ceremonies I have conducted. Once, I took the hit to be a sign of my father's death. It happened during a ceremony that I conducted a few days before his passing, and it struck me as a strong pinch in the kidneys.

The women started building the fire. I would observe and learn the process in the months to follow until I was confident that I could build it correctly myself. With a bag of white sugar Sebastiana drew the glyph of the nawal Toj in the pit. In its center, she placed a two-pound cube of pressed raw sugar, and around it we placed pom, or incense, in this case in the form of flat balls pressed from resin. Against the sugar block Sebastiana leaned bundles of candles in colors corresponding to their orientation. Red candles to the east for earth and life, yellow to the south as the incarnation of fire, white to the north for air and inspiration, and black to the west for the ancestors, water, and death. Around the block, she placed pressed pieces of pine wood and incense. On other days, these items would be accompanied by other beautiful and fragrant natural things, such as flower petals, fruit, and chocolate, depending on personal inspiration.

As we built the fire, we thought of where the items for sacrifice had come from. Someone had picked those flowers and pressed the incense. This connected us to the surroundings, our purpose, and our task. Mainly though, we thought of the person and the issue that this ceremony was for.

North and South American Indians use musical instruments to draw the numinous powers to the ceremony. The Maya are a more inward, quiet people. I have seldom encountered musical instruments, other than in official ceremonies, for which ritual musicians, such as a marimba player, a chirimia player, and frequently a drummer are contracted. Also, the ajq'ij will often blow a conch shell to symbolize the alpha and omega of time.

Using a publication that showed past Maya calendar years, we established what my energy sign at birth was. This day sign is the energy that governs a person throughout his lifetime. The women kissed the earth before the fire pit three times, and I watched as Nana Tomasa lit the fire. The women started calling upon the numinous powers in a mix of Quiché and Spanish (so that I could understand): "Uk'u'x Caj, Uk'u'x Ulew" (Heart of Sky, Heart of Earth), from sunrise to sunset. They called upon the four cardinal points or directions; the Ancestral Grandparents, Xpiyacoc and Xmukané; and, gradually, all the planets, saints, mountains, and bodies of water; the nawales; and the ancestors.

By invoking all of these forces with which human beings share the universe, we connected with them, brought them to life, and ultimately opened up communication. By thinking of oneself in this bigger picture, one disappears. One melts into space. The individual, with her daily problems and egoistic intentions, vanishes. In relation to the universe, we are small. In ceremony, everything we are and have we give back to Ahau. Ahau is God in an all-encompassing way.

Much of the ceremony was spoken in Quiché, and so day by day I would be learning some of the language. There was no need for drugs;

drugs are a quick fix. Here all connection is made by counting day energies and giving prayer and offerings. Nothing is done without showing gratitude as well.

The women prayed for me, for their friend in Germany who had asked for their help, and for their town. They asked for the blessing of all saints, which we called on by name. They called upon their ancestors and the ancestors of their nation or their people. Then they started counting the twenty nawales—and each of their frequencies, from one to thirteen—in their order on the calendar, always starting with the present day. As they invoked, they offered flower petals, rosemary twigs, sesame seeds, chocolate, and corresponding candles into the fire. With the exception of nice-smelling pine wood, my nanas never use wood for a better burning fire. Only sacred items are burned. The choice of which items to sacrifice is mostly left to one's creativity. The smallest plants can be of great power. What counts is that everything is beautiful and sweet smelling.

Blood is still the most personal sacrifice used, though I've never seen anyone do so, as that would only be done for one's very personal ceremony. I am sure, though, that Don Tomás sacrifices blood, because a vein in his knee was once infected, which caused a big upheaval in the administration, as if it were a bad sign. I believe it is where he pinches himself to let blood drop into the fire, as the ancients did. It makes sense, since with its DNA information blood is the ultimate personal substance to use to truly connect the here and there. No words are needed; the human essence and its condition at the time of sacrifice speaks for itself.

Fire, like the sun, makes the blood "cook" inside the body. From personal experience, I know that blood is received eagerly by the fire and can be extremely effective. It is a known fact that the ancient Maya as well as many other cultures sacrificed people to elicit a strong response from the numinous powers.

In today's more civilized life in the Maya mountains, animals are sacrificed instead of humans, though only occasionally at important events. On the day of my initiation, a bird should have been sacrificed, but I refused.

Sometimes, counting one nawal, the fire is very lively, while with other nawales it may suddenly diminish or disappear completely. The fire has different colors and shapes and tends to burn in different directions. All those features have different meanings, and the ajq'ij knows how to interpret them.

The ceremony took a little more than an hour to complete. At one point, a strong wind came and blew the fire, and Pilar deduced from it that I stood close to the wind, the energy of inspiration and the deities. Quite a bit of material used in the fire remained at the end, and Nana Tomasa said that usually with other participants "the fire eats it all up."

Gradually, throughout my training and beyond, I would get to experience things that would help me to understand the subtleties of the numinous world that often cannot be described by words alone. Some of them I share in this book. I would also learn that a critical mind is good, but a trusting heart is better. Following this Maya teaching and the experience since then has taught me that the Western system of critical thinking that we were brought up with can be very unhealthy—physically as well as emotionally—in relation to ourselves and to other people with whom we share life on this planet. Trust is an important capability that all of us naturally possess when we come to this planet, but in the process of living, we learn to suppress it. And so, many of us need to relearn to be trusting and trustworthy human beings. (For a photo of me preparing ceremonial materials at Nana Tomasa's house, see plate 19.)

After the fire went out, the women said closing prayers and drew a cross through the ashes to finalize the act. They kissed the earth three times, and I followed suit. We cleaned up the pit and neatly gathered mats and baskets with the remaining seeds and candles and took them to the altar room, where they would be stored. We set the long table, and the daughter-in-law and granddaughters brought in a pot of beef soup with boiled carrots and other root vegetables, along with corn tamales broiled in banana leaves. Everyone served themselves tamales from the bowl. I felt so purified from the fire that I was unable to eat any meat. I had a hard time eating anything in fact—let alone consuming alcohol—for most of the following weeks, so I stuck with eating vegetables and tamales.

We talked casually, and I met Elizabeth, another student. She was from the state of Washington and was staying with them. Nana Tomasa's ten-year-old grandson came to show me a picture he drew with the colored pens I gave him. Later, Nana Tomasa and I talked for a while, and she taught me some things about maintaining good health. Then some of her patients came to see her, so I said good-bye and left for town. I would be back tomorrow. My training had begun.

At the town center I paid a visit to the two Maya administration offices, and Julian told me about the new priest. He said that the priest was educated in Mexico and grew up in Chichicastenango. Julian shrugged his shoulders and told me that like so many others before him, this priest, too, would try to eliminate the Maya traditions, but he wouldn't succeed either.

Julian was very happy to see me, greeting me as a friend. He lamented that I hadn't come a few days earlier when I could have joined them in the celebration of one of the town's patrons, San José, as well as in the Bendición de Semilla, the Blessing of the Seed, held in the village of Chucojom. This important three-day celebration takes place during the season of planting to honor Santiago, also called the Tzijolaj, the master of the wind, to persuade him to protect the crops from storms.

The fear of crops being destroyed by a storm runs deeply. Every Quichéan community holds this feast. The village council comes to Chichicastenango, accompanied by some of their citizens, to pick up the icon of Tzijolaj from its home and take it to their community for the celebration. After circling the statue and processing through town with it, the worshippers carry it to their village, where it remains throughout the celebration until it is returned in the same ritual circling manner to its home in Chichicastenango. Many of the communities are hours away, but the walk there and back is a pilgrimage as well as a sacrifice that parishioners are willing to make.

15

THE LIFE OF SACRED FIRE AND SACRED SEEDS

March 11, 2015 (8 Tz'i')

Nana Tomasa and her daughters perform several ceremonies per day and night and are often called to clients' houses to perform ceremonies and healings there, too. Their cell phones ring frequently during the ceremonies, since they have to be left on in case another patient needs to reach them. The calls come from nearby towns and faraway foreign countries.

I was invited to live in their household during the time of my training. Although I would have liked to stay close, I decided against it. I wanted to be close to the administration and to experience life with Josefa's family. I was also exhausted after the ceremonies and needed time to myself for meditation and writing. There are a lot of children in Nana Tomasa's family, and one day much later, Nana Tomasa and Sebastiana confessed to me how difficult it is to concentrate within their busy family life.

Once again, we sat on our heels with the smoke in our eyes. We called upon 8 Tz'i', an energy that signifies law, authority, and justice. The women activated the altar by lighting the fire and calling upon the Creator: Heart of Sky, Heart of Earth from sunrise to sunset. We kissed the ground before the fire three times, and the women called the planets, the Maya grandfathers, and the four corners of the world: B'alam Qu'itzé (east; fire and the generator of life), B'alam Aq'ab' (west; the hidden force in the internal earth and the night), Majukutaj (north; air and generator of ideas), and I'qui' B'alam (south; the giver of life associated with water and nature in general).

We also invoked the town patrons and local saints, Tzijolaj, and Rilaj Mam (Maximón), as well as the ancestors, to thank them for life and for the day's energy. We began counting the nawales, starting with that day, Jun Tz'i', and called upon the characteristics of that particular day.

We prayed specifically for a patient of theirs, a pregnant woman.

The ceremonial process was fairly set every day, but the outcome wasn't. Each day, the behavior of the fire changes, and there can be other interferences, such as the wind or the appearance of animals, that provoke internal thoughts or revelations. Different messages can make an ajq'ij's blood move, which can be interpreted as being significant to the matter. Everything means something in this spiritual world, which I gradually discovered. These abilities, unused in industrialized societies, prove that it is not only one's profession, family, culture, and social engagement that give one purpose in life after all.

During the ceremony, we silently asked questions. In one instance the fire created a vortex in response, and Nana Tomasa explained how the answers work. If such a spiral turns in the direction in which the Earth's energy spins in that particular region, which in Guatemala is counterclockwise, the fire is giving an affirmative answer to one's question. If it swirls the other way, the request is not confirmed in any way by the numinous forces.

An affirmative response is also indicated if the fire moves toward the east. If the fire is pointing toward the west, one should consult the ancestors using the Tz'ité seed divination, for example. A north-pointing fire means a negative outcome. And when the fire burns high, it means that energy is being lost. A lively fire denotes a good situation.

It does not need to be big, just animated. If the flames are white, the situation shows transparency, which is considered positive. Blue-colored flames indicate an excellent outcome.

After the fire burned out, we sat and listened internally. Once the fire goes out, the smoke, too, speaks until the ceremony is finalized by the main ajq'ij. White smoke indicates a good situation for the person in question. In contrast, black smoke or ashes denote a negative outcome. Crackling represents answers that will need further definition. An ajq'ij also observes the outer influences of the wind, birds, and other unusual happenings. What mainly matters, however, is what happens within, which was what I was there to refine through daily practice. It all makes so much sense when we set aside our modern way of seeing everything as separate from nature and get back to listening to what she is saying to us.

Pilar said that she had a dream about me. In it, she saw that it would not be easy for me to encounter the entrance to the spiritual world. I remembered my own dream in which I saw a brightly lit portal leading into an even brighter light, but in the next dream vision it became clear that I first had to attend to worldly tasks. It showed me sweeping the fallen apples around the apple tree at my parents' home—an image that told me I would have to get my responsibilities in order before I could enter the light fully.

Another ajq'ij, joined us. When he found out that I did not have children, he stated, "It is not good not to have children," and went on to say that it interrupted growth. In a way, he was right. By interrupting my family heritage, be it because of political separation or otherwise, I may have denied the opportunity for others in the family to be reborn. On the other hand, I must note that his remark, I believe, also came from his experience of this homogenous, traditional society in which almost everyone has children. But there are many sides to every story, and it crossed my mind that he might have been a little envious of my free life.

I didn't tell them my personal reasons for not having children, but several days later I told them that, despite my young appearance, my time for having children was physically over, and that if this message had come from the ancestors, they should know that it was. The ajq'ij's attitude took a 180-degree turn, and he softened his tone: "Well, then, the world is your family."

Several weeks later I encountered him at an open-air concert where he asked me to buy him a drink, and then another . . . which confirmed to me that his life wasn't a happy one, children or not. Not every ajq'ij follows the mandate to lead a positive life. I remembered my friend Manuel telling me to make sure that my spiritual leaders lead a healthy and prosperous life.

After lunch that day, Nana Tomasa showed me several small woven pouches from which to choose one. She also let me choose from several semiprecious stones. Then she spilled a bunch of red seeds before me on the table and asked me to select the ones I wanted and to place 260 of them in the pouch. I spent quite some time doing that and felt a bond forming with these seeds. The next time at the fire, Nana Tomasa would pass them over the thirteen joints of my body and state that from then on they were my "husband."

The seeds are called Tz'ité, and they are used for divination and protection. (For a photo of the Tz'ité seeds, see plate 20.) After the final initiation on the last day of the process, they would become my constant companion. It would take quite some time until the nanas showed me how to work with them; it needed to be done on a specific day. The process of consulting the seeds is a secret, and I will not reveal it here. (For a description of one reading, you can see B. Tedlock 1992, 159–60.) What I can say is that each nawal, or day energy, has several meanings, which a talented ajq'ij can read, interpret, and apply to a client's situation. The ajq'ij works by asking the client questions and then interpreting the ancestor's answers by feeling her blood move and receiving insights while laying out and reading the combination of seeds that result. Insights come by thoughts, feelings, visions, or occurrences in the immediate surroundings.

Plate 1. Market in front of Chichicastenango's main church, Santo Tomás

Plate 2. Maya leader Don Tomás officiating the 2012 closing
and opening of the new Maya era

Plate 3. Ancestoral
sculptures in the
Plaza Oxlajuj B'aqtun

Plate 4. Baile de los Conquistadores

Plate 5. In the town center the Palo Volador is performed on a daily basis.

Plate 6. Dancer with Tzijolaj icon

Plate 7. Procession with icons of town patrons

Plate 8. As a sign of peace, national and international leaders put their hands together at the Oxlajuj B'aqtun celebration on December 21, 2012.

Plate 9. The icon of Tzijolaj, also called Santiago, being let down by a rope. The act symbolizes the sun turning the corner on December 21 each year, and here specifically in 2012.

Plate 10. One of four spiritual leaders performing the night ceremony
on December 23, 2012

Plate 11.
José Luis Tigüilá

Plate 12. Josefa Xijol and me in 2015

Plate 13. Personification from Baile de las Chicas, December 19, 2014

Plate 14. The Maya administration giving me a welcome ceremony. I stand with the Elders in the altar room of the Maya municipality.

Plate 15. Personification in the Baile Regional

Plate 16. Doña Tomasa Pol Suy, my teacher

Plate 17. Sebastiana Pol Suy

Plate 18. Lunch with Juana—Josefa holding up a tortilla, and Canek Xiloj in the kitchen with corn stored and hanging to dry

Plate 19. Preparing ceremonial materials at the fire pit at Doña Tomasa's house

Plate 20. Tz'ité divination seeds at Doña Tomasa's altar room

Plate 21. Doña Juana weaving

Plate 22. Baile del Torito festival, April 2015. Marc Xiloj is in lilac, facing the camera.

Plate 23. Baile del Torito festival, April 2015. Tomás Xiloj, in blue, is Josefa and Manuel's older brother. Marc, in lilac, is in the background on the right. Notice the Maya elders to the left of the image.

Plate 24. Equinox ceremony in Tecpán

Plate 25. Doña Tomasa at my consecration.
Photo by José Luis Tigüilá.

Divination is a spiritual quest and requires initiation—such as ancestral permission—preparation, and devotion. Practice improves one's ability, but talent, skill, and pure intent are even more important. I have seen people grasp the answer as if they had seen it written on the wall. Often, it is that clear. Other times, one needs to go through the process of organizing the seeds several times to come to a clear answer.

Organizing and reading the Tz'ité is a kind of language that we see reflected in the Maya glyphs that, at least regarding spiritual texts, the scribes used to write and read during a certain state of meditation or divination. The process can also be understood as the intuitive interpretation of the nawales' and ancestors' answers via the formation the seeds take when a certain question is asked.

Until my graduation, the pouch containing the Tz'ité stayed on Nana Tomasa's altar to absorb spiritual power. We only removed it from the altar to assure their presence at the fire ceremonies. I must admit that it took awhile for me to take the idea of the husband seeds seriously, and I would have preferred to have them with me at home during my training so that I could better bond with them.

As I made my way back home that evening, I felt strong, supported, and initiated to the presentation of the day energies that I would soon be keeping.

16

EMBODYING THE ENERGY OF CREATION AND TIME

March 12, 2015 (9 B'atz')

B'atz' is the first sign in the 260-day Cholq'ij calendar. The energy represents beginnings and is symbolized by a rope. It unties time and the things developing in time on Earth and in the Sky.

The day 8 B'atz' begins the Maya new year. It is the day when the first Maya were created. It is the beginning of time and space. And it is the "head" day of the Cholq'ij calendar. As the head controls the body, 8 B'atz' manages the rest of the days of the whole system of time and space. The Maya pray for Heart of Sky and Heart of Earth to come and establish themselves in B'atz' and in the people. By praying, celebrating, and engaging with this day, the Maya create a relationship between their essence and that of their source, Ahau. They identify and embody the energy of the celebrated day within their own body and function as a walking manifestation of that energy. In this way, the body is considered a sacred space.

Unlike 8 B'atz', which is a day of male energy, today, 9 B'atz' (twenty days after 8 B'atz') is the day of women and nature. The Popol Vuh states that on this day women were created. The number nine is important in Maya cosmology, particularly because it symbolizes the length of time for gestation—the nine months of the Cholq'ij calendar mirror the nine months, or moons, of human development in the womb. Nine also represents getting on the way, the road, and the energy of action.

For the Maya, time does not stand alone as a moment or as an abstract thing. They perceive it as a living entity and find in it their connection to the past and future. Within time, life develops and creates destiny, carried on by B'atz'. It is because of the concept of B'atz' that weaving is such an important endeavor in Maya life. Like DNA, B'atz' and the weaving thread alike symbolize the thread or rope that contains all of lived Maya history. Woven products often depict the structure of Maya cosmology. Through the act of weaving and in many of their patterns, women symbolize the passage of time. B'atz' is also the umbilical cord that connects humans to their source until the day they are born and, though invisible, beyond. Therefore, many American Indian and African tribes bury the umbilical cord of a child to mark the connection of birthplace and the cosmic source.

Furthermore, the Maya imagine B'atz' to hold the spiritual energy of the monkey due to a cosmological event described in the Popol Vuh. The monkey energy of B'atz' is also portrayed in the historical / mythological story described in chapter 6 of the guards who, failing to take proper care of the icon of the town's main patron, Santo Tomás, were transformed into monkeys and sent to live in the trees. From that point on, the monkeys represented a connection between the Sky and the Earth and are symbolized in the Palo Volador ritual by the flying men, who, hanging by their ankles on ropes and rotating around a tree pole, unravel time.

Invoking B'atz' at the morning ceremony, I asked the fire to unravel useless things in my life and bring in ties to meaningful and beautiful new things instead for a happy, healthy, productive, strong, secure, and radiant life fully connected to its source. Since I was born with the umbilical cord wrapped around my neck—one sign the Maya recognize as an indication of a future ajq'ij—I called for the cord to be untied so that I could enter the arch of light with clarity. I also solicited to have my eyes and heart opened to all living beings. I asked the fire to keep the telluric strings that connected me with the numinous world, brilliant and silver like the moon or golden like the sun. I felt B'atz' compelling me to move, and as I walked thirteen times around the fire, I looked for guidance an understanding and a knowledge that would help the people who would come to me for direction and advice. I felt the urge to disperse the energy and share it with my surroundings by moving my hands up and through the air as if in a dance—an impulse that moves me in almost all my ceremonies. In fact, I had felt B'atz' at 10:00 p.m. the night before, and when I got up in the morning well rested, I dressed in an orange dress and crystal necklace and exercised and danced to Sufi music.

At this morning's ceremony, Nana Tomasa joined in with me as I felt a call to move and engage in a dance around the fire. This surprised me, since I had witnessed very little extravaganza in this household or in any other ceremony at the different occasions that I had attended over the years. In pictures and videos, mainly from Tikal, I had seen acts that resembled the more expressive Maya dances and apparel described in the ancient writings. In my field research, I had seldom witnessed the reenacted dances by half-naked men with masks and feathers that supposedly imitated the authentic ancient Maya.

Today's Maya are of an introverted, rather conservative character—much more so than the people of other ethnic backgrounds. The popular Maya two-step dances, for example, are a far cry from the vivid dances of South America. In Maya ceremony, activities such as dancing are outsourced to a reserved ritual performer carrying the Tzijolaj and to the reenactors of traditional dances described earlier. Also, there is very little use of hallucinogens—an altered state is typically induced by prayer counting of the calendar days—which may make the study of this culture unattractive to an audience interested in spectacle. Jamake Highwater states that before 1850 hallucinogens were unknown to the North American Indians as well (Highwater 1982, 96).

It is, on the other hand, possible that this knowledge was lost after the Conquest and its prohibition of carrying out Maya traditions. Despite it, the Maya have tried to keep the knowledge of meaning alive through oral tradition and reenactment. However, some of the knowledge itself has surely disappeared or is still kept secret. For the Maya, though, the *meaning* is never lost even if they don't remember its origin. Rejuventation of life, the function of many rituals, is possible through accurate reenactment of their ceremonies and dances, whether or not participants know its meaning.

Our fire burned up the sugar block and the beautiful materials Sebastiana had used to create the fire for me. She had put yellow flowers and rose petals from her garden all over it. Once lit, the fire became so alive, a noticeable trait throughout all my training. I didn't know much about fire interpretation yet, but my nanas saw positive things and were surprised, since they had not seen such clarity and lightness in their students' fires before.

Sebastiana saw the animal forms of my nawales in the fire. The Maya base their personalities on the central nawal that one was born with, along with the conception sign and the destiny energy. These energies influence the nawal. With these indications, it is fairly easy to read a person's personality. Once one is familiar with these energies, one can determine which situations a person is likely to encounter during her life and what her reactions to those situations and their outcomes will be. The more one works with these energies, the stronger one's knowledge and foresight become.

Back in Chichicastenango, I accepted Josefa's invitation to a lunch meeting for clients that was being held at her office. A lunch meeting is not a simple endeavor. It is an event where a lot of food is brought in by a catering service and a marimba band is invited to provide the entertainment. I got José Luis Tigüilá, the company's director and Maya administration speaker, to dance, and being a teacher at heart, he led the way while explaining to me how to count in their language.

Later that day, I spent some time on the balcony of a café and watched a funeral procession pass by, trumpets playing mournful music. It was Thursday, a big market day, and the town was packed with vendors and buyers. Tourists had come to town for a few hours to shop for Maya handicrafts, and it felt good not to be the only white person around for a change.

17

**THE ALTAR OF PURITY
AND TRUTH**

March 13, 2015 (10 E); March 14, 2015 (11 Aj)

E is a good day for travel, so the people of the nanas' household, plus Elizabeth and I, were going to take a car trip to one of the natural altars—one that held the energy E. As explained previously, many of the altars hold one or more day energies, and people have been going to these altars to ask for favors for centuries. The altars have accumulated these spoken intentions and speak back in their own way.

We ended up not going. First, clients kept pouring in for assistance. Then, under strange circumstances, the car key got locked inside the beat-up car that I was supposed to drive. Despite my many years of driving experience, I didn't feel comfortable driving in Guatemala, so I was not upset that the key became unavailable.

So we stayed at the house, where I built the fire myself for the first time. I drew the glyph of the day's nawal with sugar, set the sugar block in the center on top of the nawal drawing and placed the candles on it. I then added rosemary twigs, pieces of chocolate, and rose petals that Sebastiana had brought for me from the yard, as well as two halves of an orange. It was a beauty. I had brought dried lavender from my mother's yard in Europe and shared it with the women to sacrifice to the fire. As usual, the smoke stung my eyes, and when I got home, I needed to wash all my clothes, by hand as is the custom in most houses where women want to stay in touch with nature. I was advised not to take a shower immediately after the fire ceremony. In fact, I often felt the need to stay smoky and therefore enveloped in the fire's spirit.

We called upon the characteristics of that particular day—E, which is the sacred way, the truthful way, and therefore considered the protector of travelers. As explained, B'atz', the first day in the calendar, begins something, and then E takes action and gets it under way. It is therefore a strong energy, a guide and leader and also a counselor, because it knows where to go. I have studied the day energies over the years and have learned much from listening and observing people here. I also learned a lot from Carlos Barrios's publication *The Book of Destiny,* which I bought at the last minute before going to the airport in 2012, and which I consider a must-read for anyone interested in the deeper meanings of Maya mystery and culture. With this foundation, I had some initial understanding of the group of meanings each sign incorporates.

While we pleased the numinous beings with exquisite fragrances and counted the days and sacrificed to them, we received messages. The messages can come in thoughts or signs, sometimes literally as the writing on the wall. A real animal may appear unexpectedly in some real but bizarre situation, or it may be supersized. More commonly, it appears in dreams. All of these situations carry certain meanings. To Westerners, it may seem like superstition, but to an experienced ajq'ij, it is a form of nonverbal language. For example, when an owl appears, something bad is about to happen in the family. To the Maya, animals have meaning beyond their mere physical existence; they carry symbols, and with those symbols come messages. There is no division between a real animal and his appearance in another form of being.

A real animal may also be a person's spirit animal, and if it is killed, the person may die also. Seeing an animal in a situation out-of-the-ordinary rips us out of our regular thought patterns and makes us able to grasp the meaning of its presence by suddenly engendering a new thought or experience. This opens one's awareness to insights.

At lunch, a couple of clients joined us with their seven-year-old son, Leonel. The boy had a brain tumor. Nana Tomasa said the parents were to get initiated as ajq'ij, but they quit halfway through the process. She saw the illness that befell their son as a tribute that the nawales charged for their unwillingness. As Nana Tomasa put it, "The nawales are possessive."

Nana Tomasa instructed me in the healing process at the fire. I had already connected with the boy over lunch when I took him to see the rabbits, and we talked about soccer and his favorite player on the Spanish "Barça" team, Messi, the world's best player at that moment. I suggested to his parents that they get him one of the rabbits as a pet.

We started the fire. Leonel stood across from me, next to his crying parents. It was a sad sight. He smiled all the time but dozed off and finally fell asleep on the ground next to the fire. There was a lot of love being transmitted between Leonel and me, and a strong bond. I wished I could heal him with this stream of love. Sebastiana approved of the movements I made to lift the energies around the fire. She nodded to me, and I could see in her smile that she liked the way I freely moved the fire.

Then we all held the little boy over the flames, and Nana Tomasa performed an egg healing on him by passing an egg over his whole body to absorb the harmful energy before burning the egg in the fire. If it exploded, the healing could be read. If it didn't, the procedure would have to be repeated. In this case, it exploded, but the reading was unclear. Sebastiana passed candles over Leonel's head, but his spirit did not improve. His eyes were deranged and he seemed "out there." We left it at that and finalized the ceremony with prayers.

MARCH 14, 2015 (11 AJ)

Aj is the energy of the sacred altar: truth, purity, integrity, rectitude, and honesty. According to Carlos Barrios, on the sacred altar Aj gathers the seven elements in unity as well—Fire, Earth, Air, Water, Heart of Sky, Heart of Earth, and the Center—representing those virtues. Aj is an especially auspicious day for sacred activities as it is the place of Ahau—a physical materialization, a place—and on this day a word or abstract thing can become sacred. On the day Aj, sacred words are spoken, and sacred knowledge is revealed. Aj is the altar that speaks the truth. Aj is the origin. Every sacred fire ground is, therefore, this origin, and this origin is multiplicable and portable. It lives in every ceremonial fire, and it is there that the ajq'ij reactivates the primordial energy.

Because the Maya see the world as integrated, they also see biological equivalents of the nawal energies in the human body. Aj is represented by the coccyx, because this is where time begins (see pages 32–33). From this starting point—which to the Hindu is the root chakra—life spirals upward, beginning as truth and transforming into its many possible facets, depending on one's decisions and circumstances.

When Aj is counted in Tz'ité seed divination, it means that truth is spoken. Glyphic writing usually mirrors this three-way process of the Tz'ité divination. The glyph Aj expresses one of the characteristics from Above or is an affirmation of the altar force, Aj. An ajq'ij receives truth from Above and so is an altar, something through which numinous powers speak.

On the day of our ceremony, Aj was in its high frequency of eleven. We each called upon our spirit animals, our nawales who sometimes come as a vision or a strong thought or a feeling inside; or eventually are perceived in the movement of one's blood. A few days earlier, my spirit energy had appeared as a vision in the ashes. Once the sacrificed elements had burned down, the energy showed itself in the form of my specific animal.

During the ceremony, while we were counting to Aj, Nana Tomasa passed a piece of pine wood over everyone's "soft spots" to absorb any negative energy and eliminate it. She touched the wood to our heads and the joints of our shoulders, elbows, wrists, hips, knees, and ankles—the body's thirteen entry points for good and bad energies. The eyes are not considered one of these doorways. Thirteen joints (including the crown as one) relate to the thirteen months of the Maya calendar.

When counting, when we arrived at Aj, Nana Tomasa passed one's pouch containing the Tz'ité seeds and crystals over one's crown. In doing so, she introduced the novice to the nawal Aj and created a connection via the seeds and stones inside the pouch to the numinous beings who in post-initiation consultations would speak to the future ajq'ij through those media. This is ultimately the most important part of the whole initiation process, as it creates a strong bond with the nawales, and in particular with Aj, the "altar," until one becomes an altar oneself. According to traditional belief, humans were laid out to be just that: a fully sacred and sanctified being. As ability develops and the connection to one's source deepens, knowledge grows, until the individual reaches the capacity to represent the cosmos on Earth. Every person does this, but the intensity and outcome vary. By working on it, the apprentice gradually opens up to Spirit and becomes at home in that world whose language he then understands. Being guided on one's true path is essential for one's life in every spiritual tradition.

After the ceremony, I left and met Josefa in town. We strolled around, buying candles at the market stall that has everything one needs for personal and official ceremonies. The candles made of tallow are thrown into the fire to honor the ancestors when calling upon the nawal day Kame. Those made of wax are for all other sacrifices. Hanging from the ceiling were seeds, pine wood, plants, and all sorts of nice-smelling incense sold in bundles of leaves or loose by the ounce, as well as images and sculptures of the saints. None of it was for tourism. Shaman-priests come there in the early morning hours to stock up on material for fire ceremonies and to adorn the altars of their houses.

Stores are built open to the street around much of the market and in neighboring streets. Once, when I realized that the women here, too, wore heeled shoes to the local dances, I wanted to buy a pair. I had left mine in New York City, bringing with me only the shoes I would wear to walk the earthy roads. But up in the highlands, you cannot find shoes for white women; shoe sizes only go to size 7 at the most.

The walls of one shop were stocked floor to ceiling with multicolored bundles of woven material. Here, Josefa chose beautiful colored weaving threads for her new huipil. We also bought flowers in the market and took them to Josefa's family grave in the cemetery.

The family tomb was painted white, and it looked beautiful adorned by the roses we brought. Over and over again a candle that we tried to light got blown out by strong wind. We spent a moment in devotion and cleaned up the family grave.

The cemetery is located a short walk down and up a hill at the western end of town. The graves are white or painted with a pastel color. Originally, people used to color them light blue for a man and pink for a woman, but now people are less strict, and additional colors have come into fashion. From this elevated place the view opens back toward the houses of the southwestern part of Chichicastenango. Josefa later took me into these private alleys. We walked through the narrow walkways of packed earth and got to the edge of the gorge that surrounds the town like a fortress. The view of the mountain across the gorge shows the road out of town where we see the buses racing up toward the capital.

On the way, we passed the house where Saint Thomas and Tzijolaj were kept that year. At this point in the calendar, Santo Tomás, together with the other two icons of patrons San José and San Sebastian, had already been taken to the main church. But Tzijolaj remained at the house. He is taken out only during the festivities when he is danced with and descends from the bell tower.

We crossed the dirt patio and entered the shack where the icons were kept. The room was full of burning candles. I saw the icon in its shrine, guarded by three men. I had heard that in the past, Tzijolaj had been stolen. When it happened the icon must have been an antique.

Being of high monetary value, it was probably sold and later appeared in a man's house in the United States. As the story goes, the man experienced bad dreams and feelings until he could not bear them any longer and brought the icon back home to Guatemala. Now, the icons are watched over, day and night.

I put candles on the altar before the shrine, knelt on the ground before the vertical glass case holding the icon and stayed to meditate a bit. After a while I attempted to get up to leave, but I felt myself being pulled back by Tzijolaj, so I stayed. A boy came forward and opened the shrine so I could give an offering of some money. I raised my arm, and a lightning-like energy struck me and ran up through my arm. I placed the offering in the wooden icon's horse and then kissed my hand and touched the horse with it. When I did so, a beam of sunlight came through the tiny western window and lit up Tzijolaj's face. It seemed like he was giving me a smile.

Magic happens all the time in this land. It is this connection to nature and its representations that distinguishes countries like Guatemala from the industrialized world of fragmentation and controlling rationality.

The empowering energy stayed in my arm until we visited the Calvary church, some time later. We ascended the stairs, and when we passed the threshold, the precious energy suddenly shot out of me and into the ground. Calvary churches are associated with death, and this one may have had underworld energies that I was not prepared to manage.

I left the church and waited for Josefa outside. Looking over at the main church, Santo Tomás, at the eastern end of the plaza, I saw the cofrades (brothers of the brotherhood) taking the floats with the three patron icons into the church. Josefa and I walked over to pay tribute to the saints, as is usual at this time before Easter.

We entered just as the cofrades were placing the icons on the eastern side of the church. I greeted Don Manuel Choc, the master of ceremonies and director of all the traditional festivities. Josefa and I set some of our candles onto the Maya ancestor altar located on the ground. We said a prayer, and I stuck some money on the colorful clothing of Santo Tomás and some other icons.

Besides the three main patrons, there are many other icons: Jesus carrying the cross; San Pedro, whom I don't much relate to; and a statue wearing a papal tiara on his head and holding a big wooden cross before him. His eyes were impressive, almost alive, and so was his vibe. I lit a candle before this Santo Espiritu (Holy Spirit).

At the front of the church some people gathered for a little mass being conducted by the new priest. It was he who wanted to rid the church of all those "other" saint icons and the customs that the Maya perform to keep them alive. And I mean alive, because make no mistake, when you put energy into a thing, beware, because you just might get a response.

Here, far from the secularized world in which I grew up, I encountered a world of marvel, living nature, and people as a part of it all. The numinous world is not for lazy individuals—it wants you to be attentive—but if you are, the rewards are, well, miraculous.

18

**THE DARKNESS AND
THE LIGHT**

March 15, 2015 (12 I'x); March 16, 2015 (13 Tz'ikin)

At 6.30 a.m. on 12 I'x, a car picked me up at Josefa's home. In it were Nana Tomasa, Sebastiana, Pilar and her husband, Elizabeth—the girl from Washington State—and Amalia, a warm woman of Spanish origin turned Maya ajq'ij, whom I hadn't met before. We drove up the road toward the capital for about five miles and then turned onto a dirt road and drove for about another mile up the mountain to a place with I'x energy. There, we met with the sick boy, Leonel, and his parents and another couple from Chichicastenango. Leonel lit up when he saw me, and he told me about the two rabbits from Nana Tomasa's yard that his parents had gotten for him. He called them Jony and Hector, after his best friends back home.

We came to this mountain spot because that day's energy was I'x. This day sign stands for the Earth and all the forces within the Earth, especially those in what's considered the underworld. To persuade these forces, a person must be strong. Those born on this day are destined to become the kind of ajq'ij who will be able to communicate with the forces that live in the darkness. Their spirit animal is the particularly astute and tuned-in jaguar.

Led by Nana Tomasa, we performed the ceremony. Everyone had brought large baskets full of ingredients to be sacrificed to the fire, honoring the twenty nawales and, mainly, the planet that sustained us. This day also held energy that was able to shift away the negative, and we were hoping to do good for Leonel. I had more space to move here. Somehow, the habit of moving my arms to lift the energies had stuck with me. Leonel, across from me, seemed to like it as well and started doing it along with me, smiling and laughing happily. Here on top of the mountain, the fire could be made larger than at Nana Tomasa's home. Flames and smoke reached into the sky as the sun rose to begin the day. The bigger the group of people, the more energy they offer to the fire. Everyone was very present on this day of high magic. It was a day of introspection, and each of us was there with his or her hopes and needs, and their own personal way of praying. If we would be able to help Leonel remained to be seen. Healing is sometimes immediate, but other times, it can be a long process that ultimately the boy's parents weren't going to accept. In a few days, Nana Tomasa would tell me that the parents had decided not to trust in the ancestral ways of healing and prepared for an operation at the hospital in a nearby town.

We got back to town around noon, and I went to visit Diego Ventura Puac-Coyoy, director of EspacioCe, Chichicastenango's first art gallery. I was looking forward to some intellectual talk. Diego is a published writer-poet and art restorer. He is very knowledgeable about the arts and conducts lectures in his field. Since he frequently goes back and forth between the capital and his home of Quetzaltenango, we made plans to meet up the following week.

Later, I was sitting on the balcony of the restaurant, returning somewhat to my Western self, when I saw Don Tomás pass by with his entourage, seemingly headed for the Hotel Santo Tomás. I could tell that he was on official business, so I did not call to him to say hello. Instead, I decided to stop by the hotel later on. I waited until after the lunch hour and then walked a few blocks through the market stalls and past the main road for cars, which at times is packed with trucks and buses that inundate everything nearby with exhaust. When I got to the hotel, the security guard greeted me. He knew me from the many official visits I had accompanied Don Tomás on over the past years.

Don Tomás seemed not to know that I was in town. Usually, everyone who visited announced themselves to the authorities—which I had, but it seemed nobody had told him, since I was not their invitee this time. (Nowadays, the custom of presenting oneself to the authorities is considered too traditional and impossible to keep since so many people pass through.) Perhaps Don Tomás had wanted to give me an official welcome. Whatever the reason, the look on his face and toward his team was somewhat reproachful when one of them told him that I had come a week ago. They were sitting with national representatives from Guatemala City, so I didn't want to hold them up. After they introduced me, and we had a brief but friendly exchange, I excused myself.

On the steps of the hotel, a street vendor tried to sell me a Maya "antique." In fact, many little antique sculptures and such can be found in certain parts of the countryside, but the ones he offered me were new and made to look like antiques. He also had rocks, so I broke down and bought a small, tourist-priced piece of obsidian and a clay figure resembling a wildcat, both for my ritual pouch. I don't know what happened to that rock, but in the following weeks, large pieces of obsidian would find their way to me as gifts, and in a way I found it more natural for them to come to me.

On market days, the place literally overflows with those antique pieces and all the other items for sale, and trucks coming from the coast bring up mountains of pineapple and shrimp to be sold in the highlands. I inquired about the wholesale prices for the elaborately designed, multicolored bracelets and necklaces offered that day. I love beading myself for its creativity and meditative aspects. Profound things happen to you when you are making jewelry. It is like a pagan activity that connects you to the spiritual world, one that was eliminated from our lives in such a violent manner that sadly most women find it pointless or unsophisticated to be involved in any handicraft. I am lucky to have had a mother who was a full-time professional and still found the time and interest to sew, cook, and teach me and my sister so many things that throughout our lives have kept us grounded and connected to the source.

MARCH 16, 2015 (13 TZ'IKIN)

Once again, on the sacred ground under the tin roof of Nana Tomasa's patio, we activated the altar with our daily ceremony. There was some light rain, considered a positive fertile sign from the heavens, and the sun wasn't supposed to come out until noon. The fire was lively, and even the smoke spoke, and I started to feel the fire responding to my hand's movements as I attempted to harmonize and lift the energies. It was the day 13 Tz'ikin, the day of the sun's authority on Earth. Tz'ikin, the beautiful free messenger bird of treasure, brings luck in money, art, and love. Often he is compared to the rare long-tailed red-and-green bird of the Guatemalan tropics, known as the quetzal. He represents the sacred vision, transmitted mainly through dreams. As the intermediary between Earth and Sky, Tz'ikin interprets higher knowledge. He may also correspond to the Christian messenger, archangel Gabriel.

The paint in the room that I slept in at Josefa's house was coming off the walls because of the humidity from the next-door bathroom. I had noticed shapes on that wall before, but that morning there was a clear image of a bird and another one of a dog or fox. Intuitively, I knew that they were the nawales Tz'ikin and Tz'i'. They would remain there for all of my stay in Chichicastenango. Other shapes, such as hearts and so on, would appear and disappear, and further magical things would happen in that room and house.

19

THE WEAVING OF TRADITION

March 17, 2015 (1 Ajmaq); March 18, 2015 (2 No'j)

The day of 1 Ajmaq, the day of the ancestors, was to be one of low-frequency nawales. My initiations with the coming nawales were therefore put on hold until the next cycle brought a higher frequency. Until then I was relieved from the daily ceremonies and teachings, so I took a vacation, which meant that I learned more about life in the Maya highlands.

Josefa and I took another trip to her family's property in the village of Camanchaj. We first went to the room where they all grew up, which was the ancestral room, and placed the beautiful white calla flowers and candles we brought from the market in the glass vase on the ground and prayed for the family and their families. The sun shone in through the southern window. In the kitchen, Juana prepared tamales and oatmeal for lunch, as well as eggs in crushed tomato sauce. After lunch we had sweet bread with coffee. I had brought a papaya from Chichicastenango, and we sliced and ate that too. Josefa's older sister, Tomasa, joined us. I had met her several times before at the house in the town center, but she never talked much. That day, though, she spoke about her husband's stroke freely in front of me, as if I belonged to the household.

Juana threw some of the remaining corn mass to the little sad-looking cat, the dog, and the six-week-old turkey chicks on the patio. I played with the cat and dog for a while, but the cat made Juana nervous, so she moved him into the kitchen, where he sat on the wood-burning stove.

The rooster wouldn't stop crowing. He reminded me of a rooster on a plantation I once visited at the Guatemalan Pacific coast that had made himself look bigger than he was and crowed incessantly while running around the hens. He was the boss. At least, he made sure it looked that way.

To start her weaving, Juana took out two sticks and with a rope tied them to one of the wooden poles that held the tiled roof to the house. She put down a mat on the patio ground and knelt in the traditional Maya way of sitting on the heels. Because they practice sitting in this position from early childhood on, people here have no problem enduring it for long periods of time. It is a way of staying in touch with the ground and keeping the spine straight to allow the energy to flow naturally.

Juana tied a third stick around her waist with a rope, so that it was in front of her on her knees. It served as the base on which she connected the threads to the upper sticks. She interspersed two thinner sticks into the threads horizontally between the poles to keep the threads tight and separated. Having done this, she tied a thread to another, thinner stick, biting the thread off with her teeth. This stick would carry the thread horizontally through the threads running to the upper pole. She slapped what would become the piece of woven material to even it out and measured the width with her beautiful, filled-with-life-experience hand. She looked over at the chicks, who were peeping and chasing each other around the patio, and made bird-like sounds at them, her long gray-black ponytail lying on the vibrant flower-embroidered huipil she wore. (For a photo Doña Juana weaving, see plate 21.)

Tying two sticks to a pole—that is how easily a weaving frame is built. Women can kneel and weave anywhere—outside their homes or by the road, their frame tied to a tree. They weave the traditional belts that protect the kidneys from the wind. They also fabricate dresses of many colors that are rich in meaning, for themselves and their families, as well as tablecloths, napkins, and such for their home and sometimes to sell. The Maya are tradespeople. In contrast to our free-market societies, however, which seem to buy products made anywhere but at home, the Maya make as many of their own things at home as possible, for it is in this unfragmented world where their strength, identity, integrity, love, and thankfulness are rooted.

A neighbor walked onto the patio, admiring the *pollitos,* the little chicks. The two women spoke in Quiché to each other, the only Spanish word they used was *material,* for "weaving." I stayed about an hour, until the sun started to vanish behind the hill. Josefa and her sister had left long ago. I hugged Juana dearly before I, too, left. Although we could not speak a word to each other, I felt close to her since she had shared her home with me and taught me about the ancient way of weaving that the Maya (and people on the European continent) had engaged in long before designers started claiming the special right to create apparel.

MARCH 18, 2015 (2 NO'J)

A night of intense dreams lay behind me. I could not step out of the house and into the world without people looking at me, and me looking back at them, engaging, thinking, writing, absorbing, and channeling all the time. Interacting in a foreign language, having to be more pro-active than I might be in my own environment, and dealing with the large families where everyone was curious and asked a lot of questions wore on me. I was as much a messenger from another culture to them as they were to me. In addition, the long, dynamic ceremonies in the early or late hours with so much to observe and learn weighed on me. I was exhausted from absorbing new things and decided to take a day of rest from it all.

Originally, I was going to use that day of wisdom (No'j) to join the meeting of the Grand Council of the Elders, but the words that I had prepared to say would have come across as weak and unconvincing. So instead, I took a walk to the corner store to buy more phone time and then returned to the house, where I passed the day alone. I took the dining table out onto the patio and, under the quad of sky that the walls enclose, I spent the day making jewelry and reconnecting to the Above. I saw an apparently sick little frog that reminded me of Leonel and seemed to be giving me sad messages about the boy, who was at the hospital in a nearby town. I washed my laundry in the outdoor sink, filling it up with water from the hose, and I baked some veggies in the oven that later on Josefa and I would have for dinner while she told me about the *ensayos*.

The ensayos are rehearsals of traditional dances, performed at certain festivities throughout the calendar year. The Baile del Torito is one of the more important ones. It is enacted yearly between October 30 and November 3 during the time of Todos Santos (All Saints), when people commemorate their deceased ancestors and saints. The dancers' training begins after Easter and is a ritual of sequences. People decide voluntarily to undergo the strenuous and timely regiment as a form of purification and a way to feel close to the ancestors whom they depict in the dance.

Josefa's nephew Marc was going to dance at the ensayo of the Baile del Torito, and he and his mother, Manuela, came over to officially invite us to be their guests. As a symbol of his invitation he handed us each a beer can, as was tradition. Marc had also brought two videos of the other dances in which he had previously participated, and we watched them both. (For a photo of the ensayo of the Baile del Torito, see plates 22 and 23.)

Another such dance is the Baile de los Mexicanos. As with all these dances, this too is based on a once real-time narrative that turned mythical. It is kept alive by repeating it in a dance every year, so there is no need for a photographic or written archive to keep it from being forgotten. The dance depicts a story of some Mexicans who came to Chichicastenango, where Santo Tomás appeared before them and performed some kind of a miracle for them, such as creating prosperity in their lives.

The forty-eight men attired in Mexican *campesino* (peasant farmer) outfits each dance to the rhythm of the marimba while carrying a live snake around their hand or neck, signifying Kan. To obtain the snakes, the spiritual guide uses prayer to call the animals in from the wild. Then he trains them in his house for one year. They are then used in the ritual dance before being freed into the wild the following December.

Marc explained the process of embodiment and how, as a dancer, one literally becomes the figure he personifies. The long training process, the ensayo performances, which the guests attend, and the final performance create a strong sense of identification. Marc described the process as a spiritual experience, in which "you go right up"—meaning out of the body and into the numinous, symbolic sphere.

Throughout their lives, most Masheños get involved in the many diverse traditional tasks. You can be sure that whomever you talk to—man, woman, or child—will have experienced, either directly or through public involvement, a spiritual connection to their source and the numinous powers. This is the purpose of tradition. It takes effort to be connected, and it is not for everyone. Most people learn it as children through prayer within their family and community, and they all do their part to reaffirm the tradition. They sacrifice and exert themselves for their higher existence.

20

≡⫼≡⫼≡⫼≡ ⫼≡⫼≡⫼≡⫼≡

THE PROMISE OF SPRING

March 19, 2015 (3 Tijax); March 20, 2015 (4 Kawoq);
March 21, 2015, the equinox (5 Ajpu); March 22, 2015
(6 Imox); March 23, 2015 (7 Iq'); March 24, 2015 (8 Aq'ab'al)

On his way from the capital to the town of Nebaj, which lay another seventy miles north in the mountains, Josefa's ex-husband stopped by the house and the three of us had breakfast together. He worked for the nongovernmental organization Semilla del Sol, which installed solar energy water pumps in remote villages. In some villages, like Santa Clara, he said, these projects were running successfully; in others, however, even the church opposed them. The Guatemalan government does not finance these alternative initiatives and takes no responsibility for supplying these villages with energy otherwise. Instead, they sell the energy gained from Guatemala's waterfalls and lakes to the neighboring countries, Mexico and Belize.

The night before, Josefa's sister Manuela had invited me to visit her school where she is a teacher. At 9:30 a.m. I walked up the hill and eventually found the school building. Kids made fun of me while I waited in front of the gate for Manuela. The elementary school was built by and named after the philanthropist Flavio Rodas. A few days later, I would meet Mr. Rodas's grandson and find out that white folks were not considered all bad and that, like my own grandfather in Europe, Flavio Rodas did not just build a school but also helped a lot of other people.

The school now receives funds mainly from a Californian couple. The teachers bring these donors up to date about the school, give them gifts as the children perform dances, and hold thank-you speeches.

If you have ever visited a school during operating hours, you know that any visitor is a hit for bringing a welcome change to the school routine. The kids jumping around the courtyard were thrilled to see me. A few asked for gifts, already used to white visitors. Many of them had been taught racism at home and carried it into the school. Most of them, though, just wanted to hug me. In her class, the teacher had them show off their knowledge to the foreign visitor, and the girls curiously checked out my outfit.

Afterward, I went to have some alone time at Café San Pasqual. The young waiter, dressed in a black and white uniform, brought me my favorite drink—hot chocolate, which is the drink that the Maya prefer to coffee. The word *cacao,* known internationally, may derive from Jun Qu'quau, meaning "First Being," which I believe is written today as Ahau and meaning "God."

MARCH 20, 2015 (4 KAWOQ)

I went back to the school for the day to attend another festivity, which felt fitting as 4 Kawoq is the day of family and groups in general.

In the evening, Josefa's sister Juana, herself a shaman-priestess, took me to her friend's house to prepare for the next day's equinox celebration, which they had invited me to. We brought materials and performed a nice ceremony on the top of a hill on her property in Chichicastenango.

MARCH 21, 2015 (5 AJPU—THE EQUINOX)

At 7:30 a.m. on this day of the appearance of God and the sun, I drove with Juana Xiloj to Tecpán where the ceremony would be held. Once there we met several ajq'ijab and participants, some from Lake Atitlan. It was quickly apparent that some from this group were what Don Tomás's people called "the intellectuals." Educated at the capital's universities, they held a somewhat different view of the costumbres than the Elders did. Not all of them had reached the age of fifty-two, which made a person "four times a person" (4 × 13 years of age) and, according to the ancestral tradition, enabled him to become ajq'ij. Nobody younger than fifty-two years old was supposed to be initiated. That went for me as well, and honestly, I didn't quite feel right about breaking the ancestral rule, and I planned to lay low until I reached the age of fifty-two.

Just as the Elders looked suspiciously at *tat* (father) Dimitri Camey for being an intellectual, he looked at me for being a foreigner in their midst. Traditional rules and freewheeling minds could intertwine, but not always in an easy or open-minded manner. Father Camey conducted the ceremony in a very serious way, but at the end, when people danced around the fire and grounds, things lightened up a little, as would be expected in a spring equinox celebration, which was intended to dispel the effects of winter and death and inspire hope for a fertile and productive year. (For a photo of this ceremony, see plate 24.)

Back in Chichicastenango, the Christian period of Lent had taken over the town. That night, young men carried the statue of Christ (*la imagen*) on a float through the dark streets, while girls carried the Blessed Virgin Mary. It is a custom where the young people laughingly suffer under the weight of the heavy wooden platforms, and in the fun and suffering, share the power of the experience. With twenty people on each side, they walk at a slow pace, sweating from carrying their heavy platform. They take a few steady steps and then, once faltering, new volunteers replace them to carry the float. Eventually, the holy image reaches the church.

The continuous processions in the liturgical calendar embody the faithful's pilgrimage, be it toward God, the sun, or the light in general. They also serve to harmonize the community in one common goal, and, through piety, to harmonize man with the cosmos he lives in.

In the Maya mountains however, the Christian import seems like a pagan celebration. Consciously or not, what the Maya really celebrate at this time of the year is Wayeb, the sacred thirteenth "appendix month" that consists of only 5 days, which, when added to the 360-day Haab calendar (18 months of 20 days each), makes up a total of 365 days. With the end of this short month, a new "year carrier" begins, and so these sacred days of the Wayeb serve as a preparation for what is to come in the new year. Shaman-priests all over the Maya region undergo a spiritual cleansing. They abstain from food, bad behavior such as anger, and sexual encounters. They meditate, evaluate, make generous offerings, and ask to be pardoned, and they pray for and about the new energy that will reign the following year. It is believed that what one does in those five days, will determine one's destiny for the year to come. Ahau's will also manifests itself in those five days. Therefore, one can rectify one's mistakes at this time as well.

The traditional Maya never go into the future without previous preparation for it. And finally, the end of the Haab calendar coincides more or less with the Catholic Easter time, so during the Conquest, to safeguard their customs and the lives of their people, the Maya Elders quietly agreed to merge the Wayeb with the Catholic tradition. The Christian Easter week embodies very much the same responsibilities as the Maya Wayeb, but many of us have just forgotten to pay attention to our own values.

The following day, March 22 (6 Imox, the day of water energy), was a day of rest for me, so I laid low.

MARCH 23, 2015 (7 IQ')

It was the day of wind. The nawales of the calendar days were once again starting to mount. On the day Iq' in its intermediate energetic frequency of seven, I continued my spiritual preparation. My day's training with Nana Tomasa and all her daughters was harmonious. We shared experiences and past visions, while my fire burned vividly. The smoke was white, a sign of peace, and beautiful in the sunlight. Nana Tomasa, wearing her turquoise jewelry and her hair down, looked rested and beautiful.

After the fire ceremony, we made arrangements for my initiation, which would take place ten days later, on the day 1 Toj. On that day, a pilgrimage of shamans from South America would be present. The group was picking up Sebastiana as the Maya representation and would later that day begin walking to Mexico, carrying the sacred rod to a shamanic council. The Ancestral Maya National Council would also be present for the historic event of officially initiating midwives into a status of authority. Midwives had never before had this official status and were legally treated as freelancers. Obtaining official status would be important for every working midwife not with respect to the Maya people but in terms of how they were seen in the eyes of the Guatemala government.

MARCH 24, 2015 (8 AQ'AB'AL)

After the morning ceremony, I met Casimiro Pixcar, a friend and representative of the authorities of the Ancestral Maya National Council. I had met him and the chief, Juan Camajay, in 2012 during the New Era celebrations.

Casimiro had come to Chichicastenango from the town of Cunén to meet with the Quiché department's Council of Midwives (Consejo de Comadronas), which represented the 665 midwives from the eighty-seven communities. The meeting was about a peculiar case that had occurred in the district hospital in Sololá, Atitlan. A newborn had disappeared out of the hospital's incubator, and the local midwife was accused of having stolen it. Apparently, another family had taken the baby, but the midwife could not prove it. The midwives district office in Chichicastenango had contacted the Ancestral Maya National Council for advice. I accompanied Casimiro to the meeting. He listened to the case and advised them on how to proceed. Really, the midwives should have first contacted Don Tomás as head of the Municipality of Chichicastenango and the district.

After the meeting, Casimiro and I walked down the dirt road to the nearby San Juan restaurant to catch up. We also called Tata Juan to say hello. I told him that we would meet him on day 1 Toj (March 30), when he would attend the midwives, and I would go through my initiation ceremony. He seemed happy.

Later on, I met with Nana Tomasa and Sebastiana, and they took me to visit the brotherhood of San Francisco, also called San Simon, or Maximón. The local saint is a patron to many people in El Quiché. Earlier in this book, I described my experiences of him when I was at Lake Atitlan. The icon of him that we visited in town seemed less real or powerful to me than the one in Santiago Atitlan, and he made no connection at first. He was housed in a little room in a house a few streets to the northeast of the town center. From the outside, the building looked like any other, and no one would ever know what was housed inside. San Francisco is disproportionately large, and his eyes were made of plastic and too big for his face. There was nothing magical about him as there had been with the Santiago de Atitlan wooden icon, dressed in scarves. But who knows. Still, we placed a candle, knelt, and spent a few moments in meditation, when I felt some energy vibrate from the icon through my body. Nana Tomasa called to leave at that moment, so I disconnected from the energy too early to get engaged and make sense of it.

21

THE MYSTERY OF
TZ'ITÉ SEEDS

March 25, 2015 (9 K'at)

K'at is the day of the net, which can either entangle you or bring in good things. Things in Guatemala can easily get entangled when a person steps out of the system of rules and customs. During the ceremony for 9 K'at, I asked the day to disentangle some things in my life. To support me, Nana Tomasa took a rope and tied two knots in it. When we came to call upon the nawal Aj, she passed the rope over my whole body, advised me to blow on it four times, and then left it next to the fire. When she passed it over me, all weight I had been feeling left me, and I felt free. I thanked her, and we continued to count the days, to pray, and be thankful.

After lunch, Nana Tomasa handed me my pouch from the altar and finally taught me how to use the Tz'ité coral tree seeds for divination. I wondered why she would do so on day K'at, but perhaps the day didn't matter and she just finally found time to teach me. It was one of the rare moments that we could spend alone. She sat across from me at the long table and looked at me with her deep eyes as she revealed to me the mystery of Maya knowledge. A world opened up before me. It was like riding a bike for the first time and thereby gaining the freedom of movement. It was like learning to read or to speak, and I was so thankful. Although there are websites that show how to throw Maya seeds, I realized that there was much more to it spiritually. It would take some time to become a good diviner, I assumed, since practice was essential. I now understood how, for centuries, archaeologists and anthropologists had been groping in the dark when it came to trying to read the Maya glyphs without the understanding of the art of divination.

Like the ogham alphabet—which probably originated in Ireland— or the Kabbalah, the Maya reading of the Tz'ité and with it much of the glyphic writing are distinct from more current forms of writing and divination. Spoken and written words can have very different powers, or frequencies. Once, in ancient civilizations, words were spoken as expressions of spiritual inspiration and actually had a much deeper intention and meaning than much of today's chatter. Words used to be taken seriously. Glyphs, too, have a different quality of meaning. There are those that describe a legacy, and those that are written from spiritual inspiration. Received in some form of ecstasy,* they need to be deciphered in their spiritual context.

The ajq'ij needs to be in a purified state to be able to receive the answers and understand their meaning correctly. He or she then has a writer or reader "paint the words," as Don Tomás once put it. In the old days, writing was not a democratic art for everybody to use; it was reserved for members of a specific profession. These languages were passed down orally to initiated scribes. Those scribes, despite their skill and importance, were mere tools. They differed from the spiritually initiated priests who communicated with the universe and could be called "diviners." Like Don Tomás today, they received the ancestral messages and then told the scribe what to put in writing.

When reading glyphs, the point cannot be stressed enough that in

---

*The term *ecstasy* is often misunderstood to mean a sort of exalted state. In reality, it means "the soul forsaking the body" (Eliade 1994, 160).

Maya life nothing is done without divination, and writing and reading are no exceptions. Only the higher beings hold the key to truth. People here always ask the advice of a shaman-priest about the situation in question. The shaman-priest then connects to his spiritual helpers and consults and interprets his Tz'ité seeds to receive answers that often are frighteningly clear. His advice is a mixture of inspiration (in the sense of communication with numinous beings) and life experience.

I will give an idea of how the divination works, but I am under oath not to go into detail about it. Although, according to Don Tomás and as published by Carlos Barrios, who cited the Tiku' prophecy described in the Book of Chilam Balam, the era of 468 years,* also known as the period of the nine underworlds or the time of darkness and silence, has ended. The Maya can now open up and share some of their knowledge (Barrios 2009, 101). This is why I feel permission to share the knowledge with you.

The person who has been initiated with the nawales—and only such a person—should, according to ancient tradition, use this method of divination with Tz'ité seeds. He is instructed to wash them with fragrance and talk to them from time to time, since they are considered to be the shaman-priest's confidant(e), the "husband" or "wife," and he carries them with him wherever he goes. Taking good care of the seeds is important for obtaining intense contact with the numinous forces.

One begins divination by thanking Heart of Sky and the Heart of Earth four times. With a purified mind, heart, and hands, one spills the well-kept seeds and stones from the pouch onto a specially dedicated piece of fabric or other material. By opening the heart, one establishes a deep connection with the seeds, or rather the forces that speak through them. Each seed embodies one of the 260 nawal energies. The more in touch with those energies the ajq'ij is, the more fruitful the answers will be. Through prayer one obtains permission to proceed. Once the connection is activated and alive, one concentrates on a question, the

---

*The era of 468 years is obtained by calculating 9 × 52.

client's question, and takes a handful of seeds without spilling any, places them on the fabric in sets of four, and then counts the twenty Cholq'ij calendar days, beginning with that day. Each group of four is one day. The last three groupings of seeds tell the answer.

There are a few other details to the setting that can be read about in Barbara Tedlock's 1992 publication. I usually repeat the process three times. By then the answer mostly reveals itself. If not, another attempt of three can be made. The connection to one's source is essential to get true results. Writing and reading the Maya glyphs, mainly of spiritual texts, also properly depends upon the shamanic outcome of a Tz'ité reading. Without ancestral approval and divinatory interpretation, there can be no outcome.

22

SNAKE INCARNATION

March 26, 2015 (10 Kan); March 27, 2015 (11 Kame)

It was day 10 Kan, and I had been feeling Kan's serpent energy since the night before when I laid in bed listening to music from my iPhone and mentally followed the musical serpent movements. We performed Kan's fire ceremony at night, and I had spent the day preparing for it by meditating and "enlightening" myself, in the sense of making myself lighter. We had about ten people around the fire, including Elizabeth, the girl from Washington, her two visiting friends, Nana Tomasa's daughters, and Pilar's husband, Carlos. The fire went well, and it was fun until I disconnected, or rather fully connected, as the serpent slipped inside of me. I felt her in my center. I had had spirits get inside my body before, but they had been people—never a snake or any other nawal.

After a while she extracted herself through my head and flew away, while physically I sat there motionless like a Buddha sculpture whose spirit had temporarily departed. The serpent—which was at that point approximately my size—flew for a while and reached the hospital where the boy Leonel laid in his bed. She got right inside him and all around his little body and his neck. She hissed out the tumor, which went flying away. She then moved through his legs, unblocking something there, before leaving and returning to my body. When I came to my senses, the fire was transparent and blue—an excellent sign, Nana Tomasa said later.

This was my first transformation into an animal. However, my personal relationship with the snake began long before coming to the land of the Maya. In 1989, the snake approached me in Karlovy Vary, the town where I was born, which I believe was my real initiation. I hadn't been to Karlovy Vary since I was a baby when we escaped Czechoslovakia to Germany. After the wall came down, I went back a few times with my parents, trips that were more memorable to them than to me. Then, one year into my studies at Munich University, I took a trip with a friend to the Karlovy Vary Film Festival. One afternoon, while he was watching one of the featured movies, I experienced my own "film." In it, I saw my mother, probably in the 1950s. She was in danger walking home at night from her job as a hotel manager.

Suddenly, she turned into me. A serpent came and circled around my throat and choked me to death. As I mentioned earlier, I was born with the umbilical cord wrapped around my neck and had a choking experience at birth. In the vision, I lay there in a rain puddle when suddenly the images turned into a cartoon. While I can imagine that the world turns into cartoons in certain drug experiences, I do not take drugs, and I hadn't been drinking alcohol at the time. In the cartoon, I was a three-to-five-year-old girl. I sat on the snake's back, and in snakelike wave movements, riding the telluric threads, we flew up into the sky until we reached the moon. There I saw a dark-skinned male face that I recognized as a Maya face. It belonged to a man I later met.

I consider this event my first initiation by a form of death and transformation, but I also experienced a calling a few weeks prior to it. It was an even more frightening experience because, besides the snake, it involved a man shooting me. I find people more frightening than animals. This second vision was no piece of cake either. Interestingly, it also happened in Karlovy Vary. Since I was born in Karlovy Vary, and assume my umbilical cord was disposed of at the hospital where I was born, perhaps it was the connection between my birthplace and the cosmic source that spurred the events that I consider my initiations, since one doesn't get initiated by a person, such as a shaman-priest, but by the nawal or spirit. Long after this event I read Mircea Eliade who wrote:

> This sky symbolism goes along with ecstatic ascents to heaven; for in many religions the candidate is believed to visit the sky, whether by his own power (for example, by climbing a rope) or carried by a snake. (2012, 159)

Since those two events, there have been other encounters with Kan, where the snake was always helpful. On other occasions, I had Maya people come to me, way before I ever went to Guatemala. One was the older Maya woman who came to me when I was teenager sick in bed. There were other early connections to Maya life as well. For instance, as a child in Europe, for Carnival, I never wanted to be a princess; I was an American Indian girl, wearing black braids, a band on my forehead, and a fringed leather dress. And from early on, I felt that I would decipher the Maya glyphs. Perhaps, spiritually and anthropologically, I am beginning to do just that now.

MARCH 27, 2015 (11 KAME)

This day I was initiated with the energy of transformation—Kame. The day 11 Kame is a mystical day with a high frequency. When I arrived at Nana Tomasa's house, she already had several clients to heal, so I had to wait a long time before we could perform my fire ceremony. Once we did, I was tired. Not much happened besides that I had two small visions of familiar images. In one I saw an altar, a crystal water glass, standing on my Guatemalan bedroom shelf surrounded by candles. The other revealed the wheel of the car that had brought me home from the ceremony the night before. It leaned against Nana Tomasa's house and was decorated with candles and flowers. After the ceremony, I trained using the Tz'ité seeds and prayed.

23

THE DAY OF THE DEER AND THE CAVE CEREMONY

March 28, 2015 (12 Kej); March 29, 2015 (13 Q'nil)

I had been up since 3:00 a.m. feeling the energy of Kej. The song "Oh Happy Day" came to mind, and I sang it wholeheartedly to myself, elevating the day over and over again. Little did I know that nine months later we would be burying my dad, singing this favorite song of his. My dad was born on day Kej, the day of the deer.* Also, when he was in the hospital, he said that he saw a deer staring at him from outside the window. And one of our strongest moments together when I was growing up involved a couple of deer. The deer is the spirit animal representation of Kej on Earth. It embodies harmony and nature, just as my father did.

Other students were present at the day's ceremony: a Maya family and Elizabeth. The fire was strong on this day of the deer in its high frequency, twelve.

The nanas left me and Elizabeth pretty much to ourselves to conduct the fire ceremony. Through daily repetition and including us in the

---

*Since the conquistadors introduced the horse to the Maya's territory, the day relates to the horse as well.

decision process and the practice of divination, they had been preparing us to lead a ceremony autonomously, and I felt confident that I had learned the process well. I had a hard time, though, talking out loud—an important part of the invocation. One should clearly say what is on one's mind and what one is asking for. I would have to learn that. Although Spanish was not my first language, it felt native to me. But how would I speak when I was back in North America or in any of the other countries that I live in, where I would have to speak in the local language with people present at my ceremony? Nonverbal communication feels so much more direct and intimate and true to me. I prefer to remain in meditation.

Sebastiana told us that seldom had they had such positive students. Usually, sooner or later, the fire brings to light a student's hidden psychological difficulties. The fire turns down many of the people who come to be initiated because of their vanity or lack of preparation or internal complications, she said. Sebastiana recommended that we always walk on the positive side of life.

I was starting to feel nostalgic, already imagining myself leaving this intense time with the women and their extraordinary generosity in granting us their knowledge, time, and love. I would miss them. I would, however, have a new world family in them, and through the fire we would be in touch always.

A client called Nana Tomasa for help after thieves had robbed her house. Nana Tomasa consulted the Tz'ité, and it turned out that the intruder was a member of the woman's own family. The very in-tune daughter of the family present at the fire could see the face of the thief and described him. The nawales also revealed that the stolen goods would be returned once the woman did the proper offerings and prayers of gratitude for her business.

MARCH 29, 2015 (13 Q'NIL)

It was 13 Q'nil. On this day of the seed one asks for what one really desires: love, family, a home, a happy prosperous job, or some other form of fulfillment. After waiting around for a while, we finally left to drive to a cave altar. We drove along the main road toward Guatemala City, and after about fifteen minutes we turned south. A dirt road took us up hills and down to the green valleys for another twenty minutes, until we reached our destination. Other people had joined us, and we were ten in total. From there, we climbed down a woodsy hill where we came upon a creek. Soon after, we arrived at the cave. It was miraculous how the more-than-seventy-year-old Nana Tomasa climbed the mountain like a young woman. We had brought baskets and bags of materials, and Nana Tomasa and Sebastiana built the fire while the rest of us went inside the cave to visit with the energies there. Somebody before us had placed a cross in the mud, and we knelt as generations of ajq'ijab had done here before us. Water drops came down from the plants on the overhanging rock above the cave, as it started to drizzle.

The nanas proclaimed it an auspicious day for planting new seeds in one's spiritual ground, and they conducted a beautiful ceremony in front of the entrance to the cave. The next day, the official part of my process to becoming ajq'ij would end with my initiation, and much of the rest of my spiritual journey would be self-taught.

24

CONSECRATION

March 30, 2015 (1 Toj); March 31, 2015 (2 Tz'i');
April 1, 2015 (3 B'atz')

The day of my consecration had arrived. I was supposed to start walking as a shaman-priestess. Would I become one on that particular day by that particular event? I doubted it. Encaminarse, "getting on one's way," was a process started long before that day, and I expected it to continue long after. The set day and event of the initiation may serve as a confirmation for the initiated individual and society, but personally I took my confidence from the things I had learned and experienced before and during the process. To me the day was far more a social demarcation than a personal one.

We were expecting my guests and the guests of Elizabeth, who would also be initiated that day, as well as the pilgrim shaman-priests from the countries south of Guatemala who were coming through on their way to Mexico, the Ancestral Maya National Council, and the Council of the Midwives. There would be about a hundred people. The midwives would move on after the fire ceremony to the altars at the archaeological site of Q'umarkaj, some twenty miles away, and the Ancestral Maya National Council's president Juan Camajay invited me to go with them.

I had paid about 400 Guatemalan quetzales for the ritual and fiesta, which included food and music. When I arrived at Nana Tomasa's house, preparations were in full swing. Tables and seating had been placed. Food preparation had been going on for hours in the kitchen and in large clay pots on an outdoor fire on the patio. Volunteers had set the tables and arranged the flowers.

In the midst of all the activity, Nana Tomasa took me aside to tell me that Leonel, the boy we were trying to heal, had died that morning in the hospital after the operation. I was devastated. He would always stay in my heart, like the embryo that I once lost, traveling with me in prayer. I realized, as I was afraid I would, that the sick frog I had seen on the patio in Josefa's house three days earlier had been a sign of Leonel's death that I had tried to ignore. The little animal had been lying there as if in a coma. And earlier that morning, three spiders had appeared in my bedroom. This unusual trio obviously meant something, but I could not concentrate on what it could have been as I was distracted by the events ahead of me. I didn't understand how my transformative experience of the snake entering Leonel's body to heal him could not have manifested his healing in reality. Toj is the day of the sacrifice, and Leonel had definitely been sacrificed for something. I had a hard time composing myself after hearing this, and as my guests started to arrive, a question tortured me: Was someone else—little Leonel—being sacrificed for me? I knew it couldn't be true, but I had felt so connected with him that I couldn't help feeling this way.

My guests were mainly members of the Xiloj family along with José Luis Tigüilá. I did not expect Don Tomás to come to Nana Tomasa's house, and I was not even sure the message of my consecration had reached him. Also, he might not have approved of it, especially since I had not yet reached the required age of fifty-two years, and I was not of Maya descent.

Elizabeth had invited several ajq'ijab from Lake Atitlan whom she had worked with in previous years. The well-known Maya shaman Don

Pedro, a Western man, would look at me suspiciously throughout the fire ceremony, perhaps wondering why I didn't come to him like other foreigners did. I introduced myself, hoping to find out who these new people were. One of the volunteering helpers looked at me with despise until Nana Tomasa's daughter Maribel told her about our close relationship, which prompted her to ask me to forgive her behavior, and we were then able to start a good conversation. Marta, Josefa's friend who wove the beautiful huipiles, also came, as did the Alvarez family, who had come with us to the cave and mountain altar. Their initiation would take place soon.

There they were before my eyes, all spiritually evolved and powerful ajq'ijab, and yet they were still not without human errors. Regardless of the preparation, training, and initiation, some egos prevailed. I could see the competition in their eyes and gestures as they greeted each other in what would seem like friendship. This initiation event was the only event that demonstrated to me the internal controversies between the ajq'ijab and how idealized reality and ordinary reality among some Maya spiritual people do not harmonize at all.

But there was also love, friendship, and support. When we began the fire ceremony, my guests Josefa and José Luis and other members of their families stood behind me. In all the mixed emotions of participants, I perceived them to have my back. I handed them pom and candles to throw into the fire.

Before we began, Nana Tomasa greeted everyone, and then to the surprise of the participants, I welcomed the people to my initiation in Quiché. In my speech, I took the opportunity to remind everyone that the Conquest had not happened only in Latin America but in Europe as well. I told them that the wisdom of the fire had been alive and well in Europe before the Inquisition decided to label people and burn them as witches. Europeans hadn't spared their own people; anyone whose beliefs differed from those of the established Christian church were made to suffer.

I could see how few of the ajq'ijab present had ever heard this point of view. Many used to secretly accuse Westerners of taking their customs and freedom. There at the fire pit, however, truth had to be spoken and words channeled strong meanings.

I knelt between the loving Sebastiana and Nana Tomasa as they initiated the fire. "Uk'u'x Caj, Uk'u'x Ulew, from sunrise to sunset," we invoked, as we had all of the previous weeks leading up to the day's finale. The ceremony was strong, and I felt strong as well. When she counted my nawal day sign, Nana Tomasa had me kneel before her and then handed me my sut and the sacred pouch holding my Tz'ité and stones. She talked to me, but I was in a daze and don't remember what she said. (For a photo of this ceremony, see plate 25.)

There were so many of us around the fire that when it came to walking around it, we were severely cramped, one up against the other, face to back. The situation felt pressurized, egotistic, and insistent. Everyone wanted to be part of the ring around the fire, and nobody opted to give way and stand aside—except me.

After the ceremony, people congratulated me. I would hold the pure happiness of my friends and the shaman-priestess visiting from Ecuador particularly dear. The photo that José Luis took of the two of us together showed the quintessence of my journey—a spiritual-cultural exchange of identities with people who could be me.

Josefa brought me a sut that her sister Tomasa had woven for me. I was so pleased. Josefa didn't know when she ordered it from her sister that I would also receive one from Nana Tomasa. Josefa's other sister Juana, the ajq'ij who took me to the solstice ceremony in Tecpán, handed me a black pouch. When I unwrapped it, a good-size piece of obsidian was revealed. I now carry it with me wherever I travel.

After the fire had been terminated, everyone was hungry. We interacted while eating the boiled meat, vegetables, and rice the nanas and I had bought in recent days and which Nana Tomasa and her daughters-in-law had prepared. I was amazed to see how Nana Tomasa, in the past few days, had calculated the required ingredients for more than a hundred people with facility, like a restaurant owner who did it every day. The *abuelita* (grandma) was deeply moved by the completion of the initiation and the end of our spiritual journey together. With tears in our eyes, we said good-bye.

Everyone left. A bus picked up the Ancestral Maya National Council's president and Casimiro with the midwives, and Casimiro signaled that I should accompany them to Q'umarkaj. Before reaching Q'umarkaj, the two buses stopped in the center of the nearby town of Santa Cruz, where Tata Juan and the representatives presented the reason for their journey to the ancient town of Q'umarkaj. Here, the Ancestral Maya National Council would, for the first time, initiate midwives to be respected as ancestral authorities, a much-needed act leading to national acceptance of their status.

As the night fell, we moved on to the ruins of Q'umarkaj. Everyone present knelt before the imposing Tojil altar-pyramid in the moonlight and prayed. The midwives and invitees had brought food and served tamales and coffee to those gathered. People were standing and sitting around the green hills that covered the ruins not yet excavated. The place, being an archaeological park, was closed, and only we were here to pass the night with another ceremony. Talking with a group of midwives, I inquired what it meant to be born with the umbilical cord around one's neck. Some didn't know, and two said that it was a sign of having the potential to be an ajq'ij or midwife.

This was when I noticed that I had lost my sacred pouch. On the first day I possessed it, I had already been stripped of it. It reminded me of the Maya myth about the loss of the Santo Tomás icon and that of the Tzijolaj. I started to panic, wondering if, after all, one of the spiritually powerful shaman-priests had arranged for the loss. I asked the mayor of Santa Cruz to take me back to town to search for it. We didn't find it. It was raining by now, and I was tired and frazzled. I didn't want to go back to Q'umarkaj as I was not prepared to spend the night outdoors in the rain. He invited me to meet his wife at his home and then generously drove me, an exhausted novice shaman-priestess, all the way back to Chichicastenango.

MARCH 31, 2015 (2 TZ'I')

It would take another week in which I would have to inquire of the icons Santo Tomás and Tzijolaj before my Tz'ité would come back to me. I received clear messages upon which I went back alone to the Santa Cruz town center and finally to Q'umarkaj, where Santo Tomás had told me to go and where I put on my sut and held my sacred vara and conducted a personal ceremony calling upon all nawales before the massive Tojil (nawal fire) altar-pyramid. I lit the candles that were left over from the previous night's ceremony. The day was hot, and while I was offering sacrifices and praying before the huge, partly excavated fire-altar, I noticed rows of ants making their way along the altar before me, carrying their eggs, which invoked the idea of my Tz'ité seeds. In a near-trance, I called each of the 260 seeds back to me and felt all of them within my being. Now I knew that the seeds were a part of me and would return to me.

I was sitting and resting on one of the hills when a man with a baby came by. We talked awhile, and then he took me to the tunnel that led inside the mountain under the altar. We passed by other tunnels, but since this walk was not for a spiritual purpose, I decided to turn around after about twenty minutes. Mainly I was worried about his baby. He said that the path went all the way to the ocean. I wondered if some people, back during the Spanish invasion of the town, managed to escape through there, while others made their way to what would become their new home, Chuwilá (Chichicastenango). Back outside, I found a calm place on an unexcavated pyramid and slept for a while. There were guards around during the day, so I felt fairly safe. I should have been protected anyway. I felt I should pick up my initiation flower crown that I had left at the Tojil altar the night before. I did so and then returned to Chichicastenango on the bus.

That night, I dreamed about the seeds. One dream involved Tata Juan, and another showed the Tz'ité coming out from under the sugar block in a ceremonial fire and flying toward me and into my chest. I was confident that they would be returned.

APRIL 1, 2015 (3 B'ATZ')

I decided to swallow my embarrassment and tell Nana Tomasa about my loss. We sat together in the altar room where I knelt before the Virgin Mary and asked for help. Nana Tomasa had just started to suggest that we consecrate new Tz'ité, at least for the days that I was still in town, when her cell phone rang. It was Sebastiana calling from the western border of Guatemala on the pilgrimage to Mexico. A midwife from Santa Cruz had called her to say that my pouch had been found. I thanked her, the Virgin, and the nawales and ancestors. Nana Tomasa and I talked about some personal entanglements in the two Maya families close to me, then I went back to town to the brotherhood of Santo Tomás, where I prayed and thanked the saint, whom I could feel put his hand over me for protection.

Without the loss of my pouch and desperately hoping for its return, I am not sure that I could have developed a bond with them. Too long did they sit on the altar at Nana Tomasa's house, removed from me through all those weeks of training and denying me any opportunity to create a bond with my so-called husband. The vara and the seeds are with me now at all times, accompanying me through airport security measures or other barriers. It rests on my altar when I'm not using it. I was also given another vara, the sacred rod that Nana Tomasa's husband had carved for me from the tree next to the altar house, and which, throughout the months before my consecration, had been sanctified on the altar by prayers.

25

WALKING AS A SHAMAN-PRIESTESS

April 2, 2015 (4 E)

My path as an initiated ajq'ij began at Nana Tomasa's fire. None of her daughters were present, and counting nawales with just the two of us turned out to be tiring. Nana Tomasa had returned late the night before from a healing in the town of Nebaj, so she fell asleep several times during the ceremony, and it was on me to continue the counting and prayers. Alone, I called upon the mountains and volcanoes and some of the surrounding altars: Pascual Abaj, Q'umarkaj, Tesoro del Molino, Iximché, Kaminaljuyú, Mixco Viejo, and the altars in the district of Petén. Once again, I called upon all the saints, the archangels, the Guatemalan San Francisco (Maximón), the patrons of Chichicastenango, and Tzijolaj. I got my first taste of the responsibility that weighs on the ajq'ij, fulfilling the daily ceremonies and serving other people. The following days would bring people to my life's doorstep, asking for help and advice. People had always opened up to me with their life's struggles, perhaps sensing my willingness to hear them out and a psychological ability to penetrate and preview situations. But only after my initiation did I feel consecrated, in every sense of the word, to give advice.

Before the day's sacred fire, I elevated the energy of the traveler (E). I took off my shoe and held my toe over the fire. I had hurt this toe walking the day before, and believe it or not, the pain went away right then and there.

Nana Tomasa invited me to join her a few days later in a ceremony that the parents of the deceased Leonel had requested for the boy. Nana Tomasa would conduct it in the ruins of Q'umarkaj, and it would be my third time before the fire-altar Tojil.

That afternoon I was invited to the first birthday celebration of Josefa's niece Chiara, which took place at the old house in town. Practically the whole Xiloj family was present. The little girl was dressed in pink, with a little white bow in her hair, and she looked like a cute doll. The women served chicken salad with tostadas, and cake on the same plate. After lunch we played something like musical chairs, where, by winning the game, I could experience my own ambition and the goal-oriented way I had grown up. It was not difficult to win. Whoever was in front of me always fixated on the next chair instead of the one they had just passed, and so sitting down on the passed chair seemed the smartest thing to do. Of course, I wasn't interested in winning, but I wasn't going to be a pushover either. Who knows, maybe they let me win.

Instead of attending the rosary prayers at church, I enjoyed several hours alone at home. I would be staying several more weeks in which I would experience more of the wonders of this beautiful people and culture.

❡

I leave you with one final thought: If some of the events described in this book sound biblical, do not be surprised or alarmed. Life is just that grand. It is much more mystical and miraculous than we normally perceive it to be. As for the Maya, their Creator wanted life to be just that mysterious and used his diverse ways of communicating to speak to us, the people. Liturgical practice of the world religions is another of the Creator's methods, but it is not the only way.

One day in the future, humans may encounter other beings inhabiting the same cosmos. If so, they may learn about the many types of communication possible and about the variety of forms life can take. May we start preparing for all of those possibilities by opening our minds and hearts today.

SELECTED BIBLIOGRAPHY

Acides Paredes, Jorge. *El Popol Vuh y la trilogía bananera: Estructura y recursos narrativos.* Newark: University of Delaware Press, 2002.

Andrade Warner, Fernando. *Popol Vuh: (Anónimo).* Mexico: Fernández editors, 1985.

Arafín-Cabo, Pressia. *Prácticas Tradicionales Maya de Resolución de Conflictos en los Territorios Kiche, Tzutujil y Kaqchikel.* Deutsche Gesellschaft für Internationale Zusammenarbeit (GIZ), 2011.

Aristotle. *Physics: Book IV.*

Bargatzky, Thomas. *Eine Einführung in die Wissenschaft von den urproduktiven Gesellschaften.* Hamburg: Buske, 1979.

Bargatzky, Thomas, et al., in a contribution by Sabine Straßer. "Das Matriarchat: Mythos oder Wirklichkeit." *IQ Wissenschaft und Forschung on Bayern 2 German Radio.* September 18, 2018, at 6:05 p.m.

Barrios, Carlos. *The Book of Destiny: Unlocking the Secrets of the Ancient Mayans and the Prophecy of 2012.* New York: HarperCollins Publishers, 2009.

Bastos, Santiago, and Aura Cumes. *Mayaización y vída cotidiána: La idiología multicultural en la sociedad guatemalteca.* Vol 1–8. Guatemala: FLACSO CIRMA, Cholsamaj, 2007.

Bell, Catherine M. *Ritual Theory, Ritual Practice.* New York: Oxford University Press, 1992.

Belting, Hans. *Likeness and Presence: A History of the Image before the Era of Art.* Translated by Edmund Jephcott. Chicago: University of Chicago Press, 1994.

Berkeley, George. *A Treatise Concerning Principles of Human Knowledge.* London: Jacob Tonson, 1734.

Bricker, Victoria Reifler. *The Indian Christ, the Indian King: The Historical Substrate of Maya Myth and Ritual.* Austin: University of Texas Press, 1981.

Bunzel, Ruth. *Chichicastenango.* Edited by José Pineda Ibarra. Guatemala: Ministerio de Educación, 1981.

Carmack, Robert. *Quichean Civilization: The Ethnohistoric, Ethnographic, and Archaeological Sources.* Berkeley: University of California Press, 1973.

Chavez, Adrián. *Pop Wuj: Libro del Tiempo.* First edition, fourth reprint. Buenos Aires: Del Sol, 2007.

Christenson, Allen J. *Popol Vuj. The Sacred Book of the Maya.* Norman: University of Oklahoma Press, 2007.

Ciudad Ruiz, Andrés, et. al. *El ritual en el mundo maya: de lo privado a lo público.* Madrid: Sociedad Española de Estudios Mayas, 2010.

Cook, Garrett W. *Renewing the Maya World: Expressive Culture in a Highland Town.* Austin: University of Texas Press, 2000.

Danz, Christian. *Die Macht des Mythos.* Edited by Werner Schüssler. Berlin: Walter, 2015.

De la Garza, Mercedes. *La consciencia histórica de los antiguos Mayas.* Mexico: UNAM, Coordinacion de Humanidades, 1975.

———. *Rostros de lo sagrado en el mundo maya.* Mexico: Paidos, 1998.

De Landa, Diego. *Yucatan Before and After the Conquest.* New York: Dover Publications, 1978.

Dowker, Fay. "Past, Present and Future: The Science of Time." Presented at the conference Time, Time, Time. Science, Art & Philosophy, Lugano, Switzerland, August 2018.

Ekern, Stener. *Comunidad y Liderazgo en la Guatemala K'iche'.* Guatemala: Cholsamaj, 2010.

Eliade, Mircea. *The Myth of Eternal Return.* Princeton, N.J.: Princeton University Press, 1991.

———. *Patterns in Comparative Religion.* Lincoln: University of Nebraska Press, 1996.

———. *Rites and Symbols of Initiation: The Mysteries of Birth and Rebirth.* New York: Harper and Row, 1958. Reprint edition Putnam, Conn.: Spring Publications, 2012.

———. *The Sacred and the Profane: The Nature of Religion.* New York: Harcourt, Brace and World, 1959.

Erkens, Franz-Reiner. "Sakral legitimierte Herrschaft im Wechsel der Zeiten und

Räume: Versuch eines Überblicks." In *Die Sakralität von Herrschaft,* edited by Franz-Reiner Erkens, 7–32. Berlin: Akademie Verlag, 2002.

Freidel, David, Linda Schele, and Joy Parker. *Maya Cosmos: Three Thousand Years on the Shaman's Path.* New York: W. Morrow, 1993.

Geertz, Clifford. *The Interpretation of Cultures.* New York: Basic Books/ HarperCollins, 1973.

Görg, Manfred. *Mythos, Glaube und Geschichte.* Düsseldorf: Patmos, 1998.

Gossen, Gary H. (ed.). *Chamulas in the World of the Sun: Time and Space in a Maya Oral Tradition.* Cambridge, Mass.: Harvard University Press, 1974.

———. *Symbol and Meaning beyond the Closed Community: Essays in Mesoamerican Ideas.* Albany, N.Y.: Institute for Mesoamerican Studies, University at Albany, 1986.

Hart, Thomas. *The Ancient Spirituality of the Modern Maya.* Albuquerque: University of New Mexico Press, 2008.

Henare, Amiria J. M., Martin Holbraad, and Sari Wastell. *Thinking Through Things: Theorising Artefacts Ethnographically.* London: Routledge, 2007.

Highwater, Jamake. *The Primal Mind.* New York: New American Library, 1982.

Hübner, Kurt. "Die moderne Mythos-Forschung—eine noch nicht erkannte Revolution." In *Wege des Mythos in der Moderne.* Edited by Dieter Borchmeyer. München: DTV, 1987.

———. *Die Wahrheit des Mythos.* München: Beck, 1985.

Ixchop Soc, Pedro. *Oraciones Maya.* Guatemala: ASMG: CRNEMG, 2010.

Jamme, Christoph, and Stefan Matuschek. *Handbuch der Mythologie.* Darmstadt: Philipp von Zabern, 2014.

Jones, Adam, ed. *Weltende.* Wiesbaden: Harrassowitz, 1999.

Jurosz-Landa, Gabriela. "Art Anthropology: Indigenous Concepts in Contemporary Art in Guatemala." *Anthropos A,* no. 109.2014/1. Fribourg, Switzerland: Academic Press, 2014.

———. *Cesta Mayů do budoucnosti.* Prague: Sféra, 2014.

———. "Die Rolle der höchsten Autorität der Maya in Guatemala." *Anthropos,* no. 111.2016. Fribourg Switzerland: Academic Press, 2016.

Kohl, Karl Heinz. "Ein verlorener Gegenstand? Zur Widerstandsfähigkeit autochthoner Religionen gegenüber dem Vordringen der Weltreligionen." In *Religionswissenschaft. Eine Einführung,* edited by Hartmut Zinser. Berlin: Dietrich Reimer Verlag, 1988.

Köpke, Wulf / Schmelz, Bernd. *Herz der Maya Guatemala.* Hamburg: Museum für Völkerkunde Hamburg, 2010.

Léon-Portilla, Miguel. *Time and Reality in Thought of the Maya.* Norman: University of Oklahoma Press, 1988.

Lerner, Jesse. *The Maya of Modernism: Art, Architecture, and Film.* Albuquerque: University of New Mexico Press, 2011.

Martin, Juan de Dios Gonzáles. *La Cosmovision indigena guatemalteca ayer y hoy.* Guatemala: Universidad Rafael Landivar. Revista Estudios Sociales, 2001.

———. *Memorias del Segundo Congreso Internacional de Mayistas.* Mexico: Universidad Autónoma de Mexico, 1995.

Medina, Tito. *El libro de la cuenta de los Nawales.* Guatemala: Fundación CEDIM, Iximulow Memorial de Sololá, 2007.

———. *Traducción al español de Simón Otzoy, revisión y notas de Jorge Luján Muñoz.* Guatemala: Comisión Interuniversitaria Guatemalteca del Descubrimiento de América, 1999.

Men, Hunbatz. *Secrets of Maya Science/Religion.* Translated by D. Gubiseh Ayala and James Jennings Dunlap II. Santa Fe: Bear & Co., 1990.

Molesky-Poz, Jean. *Contemporary Maya Spirituality: The Ancient Ways Are Not Lost.* Austin: University of Texas Press, 2006.

Moore, Robert L. *The Archetype of Initiation. Sacred Space, Ritual Process, and Personal Transformation.* Bloomington, Ind.: Xlibris Corporation, 2001.

National Council of Maya Spiritual Leaders in Guatemala (Oxlajuj Ajpop). *Ajpop Rech Nawalja Tinamit: Autoridad Ancestral Maya de Guatemala, Sistematización de Experiencias.* Guatemala: Oxlajuj Ajpop, 2008.

Neuenswander, Helen. *Estudios cognitivos del sur de Mesoamerica.* Edited by Arnold Dean. Dallas: SIL, Museum of Anthropology, 1977.

Patočka, Jan. *Přirozený svět jako filosofický problém.* Prague: Československý spisovatel, 1992.

———. *Tělo, společenství, jazyk, svět.* Prague: Oikúmené, 1995.

Peniche Barrera, Roldan. *Mitología Maya: Serpientes, gigantes y pajaros mágicos.* Merida Yucatan: Editorial Dante, 2011.

Picht, Georg. *Kunst und Mythos.* Stuttgart: Klett-Cotta, 1986.

Powell, Christopher. "The Shapes of Sacred Space." Dissertation, The University of Texas at Austin, 2010.

Puech, Henri-Charles. "Gnosis and Time." In *Man and Time. Papers from the Eranos Yearbooks,* edited by Joseph Campbell. New York: Routledge and Kegan Paul, 1958.

Rappe, Guido. *Archaische Leiberfahrung: Der Leib in der frühgriechischen Philosophie und in außereuropäischen Kulturen.* Germany: Akademie Verlag, 1995.

Ratzinger, Joseph. *Glaube und Zukunft*. München: Kösel Verlag, 1970.

Recinos, Adrian. *Popol Vuh: Las antiguas historias del Quiché*. Guatemala: Piedra Santa, 1997.

Rodas, Flavio N., Ovidio Rodas Corso, and Lawrence Faulkner Hawkins. *Chichicastenango: The Kiche Indians; Their History and Culture; Sacred Symbols of their Dress, and Textiles*. Guatemala: Unión Tipográfica, 1940.

Rössler, Marin. "Indigene Bewegungen und das Recht auf Eigenart." In *Bewegliche Horizonte: Festschrift zum 60; Geburtstag von Bernhard Streck*, edited by Katja Geisenhainer. Leipzig: Leipziger Universitätsverlag, 2005.

Schele, Linda, and Mary Ellen Miller. *The Blood of Kings: Dynasty and Ritual in Maya Art*. Fort Worth: Kimbell Art Museum, 1986.

Smithsonian National Museum of the American Indian (NMAI). "The Creation Story of the Maya." *Youtube*. June 14, 2012.

Streck, Bernhard. "Das Sakralkönigtum als archaistisches Modell." In *Die Sakralität von Herrschaft*, edited by Franz-Reiner Erkens. Berlin: Akademie, 2002.

———. "Eschatologie als Ausnahmezustand: Vorstellungen von einem Ende ohne Neuanfang in Brasilien und Melanesien." In *Weltende*, edited by A. Jones. Wiesbaden: Harrassowitz, 1999.

———. "Lynchjustiz—Oder im Schatten der Regulierten Anarchie." In *Subjekte und Systeme*, edited by Günter Best and Reinhart Kößler. Frankfurt/Main: IKO, 2000.

———. *Sterbendes Heidentum: Die Rekonstruktion der ersten Weltreligion*. Leipzig: Eudora, 2013.

Tepe, Peter, Thorsten Bachmann, Yoschiro Nakamura, and Birgit Zur Nieden, eds. *Mythologica. Düsseldorfer Jahrbuch für interdisziplinäre Mythosforschung*. Essen: Die Blaue Eule, 2002.

Tedlock, Barbara. *Time and the Highland Maya*. Albuquerque: University of New Mexico Press, 1992.

Tedlock, Dennis. trans. *Popol Vuh*. New York: Simon and Schuster, 1996.

Turner, Victor. "Body, Brain and Culture." *Zygon: Journal of Religion and Science*, 18 (1983).

———. *The Ritual Process: Structure and Anti-Structure*. Ithaca: Cornell University Press, 1969.

Viveiros de Castro, Eduardo. After-dinner speech at Anthropology and Science, the 5th Decennial Conference of the Association of Social Anthropologists of Great Britain and Commonwealth, July 14, 2003. Published in *Manchester Papers in Social Anthropology*, July, 2003.

————. "Cosmological Deixis and Amerindian Perspectivism." *Journal of the Royal Anthropological Institute,* 4, no. 3 (September 1998).

Vogt, Evon Z. "Cardinal Directions and Ceremonial Circuits in Maya and Southwestern Cosmology." *National Geographic Society Research Reports,* no. 21 (1985).

————. *Zinacantan: A Maya Community in the Highlands of Chiapas.* Cambridge, Mass.: Belknap, 1969.

von Weizsäcker, Carl Friedrich. "Kunst—Mythos—Wissenschaft." In *Wege des Mythos in der Moderne,* edited by Dieter Borchmeyer. München: DTV, 1987.

Zosi, Claudia Federica. *Consciencia maya: vivir como un ser de tiempo.* Buenos Aires: Editorial Kier, 2006.

INDEX

ABOUT THE AUTHOR

Gabriela Jurosz-Landa was born in 1966 in Czechoslovakia (now the Czech Republic). Her family escaped communism and fled to Germany when she was two years old. Growing up in Bavaria, she attended Ludwig Maximilian University in Munich where she studied art history, anthropology, and psychology and received a master of arts degree. The year after the Berlin Wall fell in 1989, Gabriela transferred to Charles University in Prague and, for the next three years, re-learned the culture of her birth. In 1992, she guided a group of American journalists into the Yugoslavian war front and had the opportunity to become a war journalist herself.

Deciding on the path of love not war, she returned to Prague to write for the German weekly paper *Prager Wochenblatt*. In 1993, she enrolled in the University of Vienna under the Maya studies professor Ferdinand Anders and visited Guatemala for the first time. Intrigued by Guatemalan art, she returned to the country for further research and ultimately lived there for six years, absorbing the culture and channeling it through painting, photography, and jewelry design. In Guatemala she opened a gallery and over the following years traveled to Europe and the United States to exhibit her work and designer collaborations, all the while keeping an anthropologic diary.

In 2001, Gabriela moved to New York City to work as an art critic and correspondent for Prague's *Atelier Art Magazine* and photograph the fast-paced and politically charged times of the Bush era post 9/11. In the following years, she earned a master's degree in anthropology and art history from the Ludwig Maximilian University of Munich and exhibited her artwork internationally. In 2012, her visions about returning to the Maya land became her destiny when she met the leader of the Maya Quiché who invited her to attend the New Era celebrations in the Guatemalan Highlands. In the following years, she spent extended periods in the country, and in 2015 was initiated as a Maya daykeeper and spiritual guide.

Her publications and lectures are based on her research in Maya traditions and philosophy, spirituality, and culture as well as in Western art including museology and city anthropology. Fluent in four languages, her articles on culture, art, and anthropology have appeared in publications around the world. She is the editor, founder, and president of the Forum of World Cultures, for which she organizes and curates international cultural-political events.

She currently resides in Connecticut, traveling and spending long stretches of time in her home cultures in both Europe and Guatemala. For more information, please visit www.Gabriela-Jurosz-Landa .jimdo.com.